CW01459487

JULIE ANN GODSON

free
SPIRITS
OF OXFORDSHIRE

• • • • • • • • • •

Twenty true lives from history

• • • • • • • • • •

Alley Cat Books

First published in 2022
© Julie Ann Godson

The author has asserted their moral right under
the Copyright, Designs and Patents Act, 1988, to be identified
as the author of this work.

All Rights reserved. No part of this publication may be reproduced,
copied, stored in a retrieval system, or transmitted, in any form or by any means,
without the prior written consent of the copyright holder, nor be otherwise circulated
in any form of binding or cover other than that in which it is published and without
a similar condition being imposed on the subsequent purchaser.

A CIP catalogue record for this title is available from the British Library.

Cover image: *A view of Oxfordshire from the south side of Headington Hill*, 1803–04,
by J M W Turner (Ashmolean Museum)

In memory of Neil Everett,
a genuine free spirit

Contents

Introduction

A FREE SPIRIT, according to the Merriam-Webster dictionary, is "a person who thinks and acts in an uninhibited way without worrying about normal social rules". But rules change over time, and one learns early on in the course of research that what might have appeared to contemporaries to be puzzling or even laughable eccentricity might actually be diagnosed today as post-traumatic stress disorder. As soon as I discover that a subject has endured military action, as so many men did, I treat their later actions with great circumspection.

Anyway, our purpose here is not to ridicule but to celebrate. The Oxfordshire characters in this collection of course vary; some lived lives of constant experiment or single-mindedness like the member of parliament who became a tramp or the son of a hatter who became a pirate, and some indulged in flashes of free spiritedness like the vicar who joined a tribe of Aboriginal Australians, or the competitive pedestrian who took advantage of a passing fashion.

Sadly, the collection features only three female free spirits, presumably because opportunities for ordinary women to leave aside domestic cares were limited. But the patience shown by the wives of the men featured is notable.

Julie Ann Godson
2022

1
The reluctant rector

ARRIVING AS THE NEW RECTOR in a country village where your predecessor has been a much-loved and popular figure can never be easy, and in Steeple Aston in the spring of 1680 Richard Duckworth certainly appears to have made as much of a hash of it as was humanly possible. Energetic, but bone-headed and lacking in empathy, Duckworth set his own agenda, regardless of the wishes and expectations of his parishioners. And he spent most of his time hiding in his rectory.

He was, however, a man of principle, a free-thinker prepared to stand up for his beliefs. At the age of nineteen he was one of only six

Duckworth's church of St Peter and St Paul in Steeple Aston

New Inn Hall, Oxford

Oxfordshire clergymen to conform to James II's *Declaration of Liberty of Conscience*. This dry-sounding initiative was actually a revolutionary and controversial move granting religious freedom for Catholics (like James), Protestant dissenters (like Duckworth), and even—most distressingly of all for many at the time—Jews and Muslims. The declaration marked an important step towards religious freedom in Britain and so, naturally, most Church of England ministers were unhappy with this attack on their monopoly.

Having graduated from New Inn Hall, Oxford, Duckworth was made Lancashire Fellow of Brasenose College, and in 1661 he became junior bursar. At various times between 1665 and 1679 he held the posts of vice-principal and senior bursar of Brasenose.

But when he was instituted rector at the church of St Peter and St Paul in Steeple Aston in March 1680, his glittering record among the dreaming spires held little sway with the good people of the village. They were more worried about his tightening up on the full payment of tithes. His regular disappearing-acts were also an irritation. Residents complained in 1682 that services were neglected and that, when Duckworth did turn up in the parish, he hid in the rectory—even on Sundays.

And the rectory certainly sounds like a very agreeable place in which to skulk. It stood west of the churchyard, well secluded from the village thoroughfares. Assessed at seven hearths in 1662, it was described in 1683 as a two-storied stone building with cocklofts (attics between the top floor and the roof). The roof was part thatched and part stone-slated. The parlour boasted handsome oak-wainscotting and a boarded floor; the kitchen rejoiced in sturdy stone flags, while the other down-stairs rooms had simple earthen floors. Outside were a slated dovecote and a thatched gate house. All together, it must have been charming.

Duckworth became embroiled in continual disputes with his parishioners. An absentee minister was fine, so long as he provided a curate to carry out the necessary offices. But, in spite of the rarity of his own appearances in church, Duckworth refused to appoint a curate.

He neglected parish customs too. It was customary for the rector to provide entertainment at christenings and to furnish cakes and ale when the inhabitants paid their modest tithes. The rector also traditionally gave a dinner on Christmas morning to all the married folk in Steeple

Looking down Paine's Hill from the direction of Duckworth's church

A seventeenth-century schoolroom

Aston, then in the evening to their children and servants. The entertainment was supposed to be repeated on Boxing Day for the inhabitants of Middle Aston. No such luck with Duckworth.

He countered complaints over these omissions by pointing out the absence of a "terrier"—the document detailing the income from Church of England lands and property in the parish by which the rector could meet his personal and parish expenses. Furthermore, felt Duckworth, his predecessors had become lax in the matter of claiming tithes, Easter offerings, and surplice fees, all of which should have formed part of his income. This neglect, he said, was what had led to the church falling in to disrepair.

He complained, too, that the parish records were in private hands; that the pulpit had been moved to the darkest corner of the church; and that the parish clerk's seat had been removed so that he was forced to lean over the back of some other seat "which caused much irreverence in divine service, others… imitating that indecent posture". One can only imagine the stifled sniggers.

While he was at Steeple Aston, Duckworth took on the duties of village schoolmaster. The school had been founded by one of Duckworth's predecessors Samuel Radcliffe in 1640. Of roughcast rubble, the building has the original stone-mullioned windows of the seventeenth century; the cartouche on the south front once displayed Radcliffe's arms, but it is now blank. At the upper west end, an oval, moulded window may be a feature of Duckworth's restoration works in 1688, works he himself commemorated in a tablet which can still be seen. (The single-bayed extension with a bellcot, and a new schoolroom on the north are later.)

Education here was for boys only, of course, and Duckworth was said to have been a competent headmaster, but severe with his scholars—some of whom were of good birth, as shocked antiquarian Thomas Hearne complained. Harsh treatment of children further down the social scale was evidently perfectly acceptable. A teacher might deal out punishment by means of a stick with birch twigs attached to it.

The school day began at 6am in summer and 7am in winter (people got up early and went to bed early in those days). Lunch was from 11am to 1pm. School finished at about 5pm. Boys went to school six days a week, with few holidays. Pupils =[learned to read and write with something called a horn-book. It was not a book in the modern sense. Instead, it was a wooden board with a han-

Steeple Aston school, founded by Duckworth's predecessor

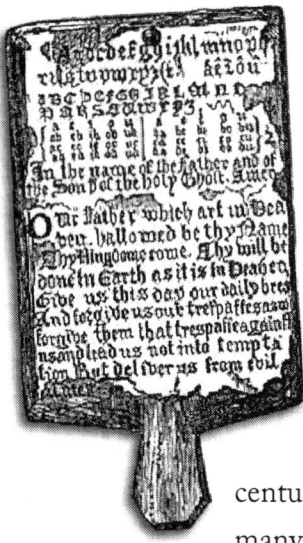

dle. Fixed to the board was a sheet of paper with the alphabet and the Lord's Prayer shown on it. The paper was usually protected by a thin slice of animal horn.

Upper-class girls (and sometimes boys) were taught by tutors. Middle-class girls might be taught by their mothers. There were also dame schools, usually run by a woman, where young girls were taught skills like reading and writing. During the seventeenth century boarding schools for girls were founded in many towns. In them, girls were taught subjects like writing, music, and needlework.

Adding to Duckworth's unpopularity was his high-handed approach towards restoring the church. Repairs were needed to the chancel but, in the absence of his proper dues, Duckworth reasoned that he would have to filch the materials from elsewhere within the building. Stone was transferred from the north aisle, leaving the congregation exposed to the elements. Props had to be installed to prevent the newly-weakened north aisle from collapsing.

As well as the church and school, Duckworth also worked to improve the parish's streets and water supply. But his most absorbing interest had little to do with the welfare, spiritual or physical, of his parishioners. Richard Duckworth was evidently deeply interested in church bells, and later reports suggest that he was a very skilled ringer.

Swinging bells to make them sound, as opposed to ringing them, was common in all British churches until at least the fifteenth century and, for most churches, right up until the eighteenth century. Stories of the power of bells to heal, to drive away evil and the devil, to calm storms and to save people from plague, pests and enemies led to bells being rung at the time of death to keep the devil away from the soul of the departed.

Seventeenth-century bell-ringing

During the decades of the Reformation from 1540 onwards, the method evolved slowly from swinging to what is now known as ringing. From about 1630 ringers in London and Norwich had been experimenting with changes, called "methods", some of which are still in use today. Due to its very high number and density of churches and monasteries, Oxford was the well-spring of many methods of ringing church bells during the seventeenth century.

The lasting legacy of Richard Duckworth is his authorship of *Tintinnalogia, or, the Art of Ringing*, published in 1668, the first book published on the art of change ringing. This difficult man's book gives a clear exposition of the state of that art at the time and, according to campanologists, was written by someone with a firm grasp of the principles and a lucid manner of explanation. It even has a final section giving advice on the hanging of bells. There are probably only two copies in existence. Demand outstripped production and a second edition, with a new title

St Alban Hall in Merton Street, Oxford

page, was published in 1671 with no alterations or additions. The only known copy of this edition is held in the Bodleian Library.

Duckworth's constant legal machinations reputedly improved the value of the living at Steeple Aston, but at the expense of his relations with his parishioners. In around 1692 he was forced to leave to become principal of St Alban Hall, now incorporated in to Merton College. The bursar of Brasenose, Dr John Houghton, described him as being "of a sower, harsh disposition and almost intolerable… Nothing, I am told, will please him."

Duckworth died on 19 July 1706 and he was buried at Steeple Aston on the following day. His rectory was demolished in 1832, and a new one built in the classical style. A fine memorial tablet was erected on the south wall of the chancel, to the right of the altar and, as the author of *Tintinnalogia*, his name is known across the United Kingdom, the USA, Australia, New Zealand—and indeed anywhere where people practise the traditional art of campanology.

2
The Woodstock pirate

WOODSTOCK SEEMS an unlikely place to produce a seadog as salty as Simon Hatley. About as far as you can get in England from any coast, the lovely little town became rich mostly on the manufacture and sale of luxury goods with which to tempt aristocratic guests staying at Blenheim Palace.

Indeed, Hatley's own father, also Symon, was a hatter and maltster who lived comfortably at 6–8 High Street. An established member of the town's prosperous merchant class, Hatley senior even became mayor of Woodstock. Drowning in respectability, therefore, he may have had interesting views on his son's decision to take the unconventional route.

Simon Hatley refused the chance to become a hatter

Woodstock grammar school stood on the site of the garden now in front of the church

Along with his younger brothers Matthew and William, Simon Hatley received a good education at the Woodstock grammar school, at that time situated in a former chantry chapel north of the church on Park Road. As the eldest boy, Simon might normally have been expected to follow his father into the family business, but perhaps learning about the exploits of heroes like Christopher Columbus, Vasco da Gama and Ferdinand Magellan fired young Simon's appetite for adventure.

Simon's brother Matthew died aged twelve in 1699, and at around the same time Simon left home for Bristol to apprentice as a pilot. At the time, the term "pilot" applied

6–8 High Street: the home Simon Hatley swapped for a life at sea

to an officer serving on board a ship during the course of a voyage and having charge of the helm and the ship's route. Nowadays it signifies a person taken on board at a certain place for the purpose of conducting a ship through a river, road or channel, or out of or in to a port.

Privateers were pirates who sailed in armed ships carrying letters of marque from their government authorising them to plunder enemy vessels, usually during a war, keeping any profits for themselves and their ships' owners—so long as they paid a cut of that bounty back to the government. The bearer of the letter of marque would then go about hiring his or her own crew and ship at their own expense. The War of the Spanish Succession (1701–1714) found Britain and Spain on opposing sides, so Spanish ships were considered by the British government to be fair game—especially if private citizens were prepared to take the risks.

Privateer and explorer William Dampier approached Captain Woodes Rogers to lead a privateering voyage against the Spanish. It consisted of two well-armed ships, *Duke* and *Duchess*, with Rogers as captain of *Duke*. Dampier, possibly the inspiration for Jonathan Swift's Lemuel Gulliver of *Gulliver's Travels*, was to serve as sailing master—a historical rank denoting a naval officer trained in and responsible for the navigation of a sailing ship. Hatley completed his formal training by 1706 at the latest, and in 1708 at the age of twenty-three, he signed on as third mate, a junior officer position, on a privateering expedition aboard *Duchess*.

Duke and *Duchess* sailed

Duchess and Duke

The Juan Fernández Islands off Chile

from Bristol on 1 August 1708. After beating their way around Cape Horn, the two vessels stopped at the Juan Fernández Islands off Chile for resupply. The islands were believed to be uninhabited, so the landing party was somewhat surprised to be met by Alexander Selkirk, a Scottish sailor who had been marooned there by his captain more than four years before. Selkirk is believed to be the model for the hero of Daniel Defoe's *Robinson Crusoe*. Rogers made Selkirk second mate on *Duke*.

After resupplying, the expedition began to raid Spanish commerce. Pirates and privateers were extremely diligent about sharing out loot fairly. To ensure equal division of the spoils, the committee of expedition members decided that each ship should appoint two agents, one to remain on the vessel, the other to transfer to the other ship. This meant that a witness could monitor what plunder was captured by the other crew. Hatley was elected an agent for *Duchess*, and transferred to *Duke*.

Thus, for a time, Hatley, who would later inspire Samuel Taylor Coleridge's albatross-slaying seaman of the *Ancient Mariner*, shared a vessel with the probable original for Daniel Defoe's *Robinson Crusoe*, plus the likely inspiration for Lemuel Gulliver of *Gulliver's Travels*.

Threatening to burn the town of Guayaquil (in present-day Ecua-

Captain Woodes' men search the ladies of Guayaquil for hidden jewels

dor), they captured several vessels while negotiating a ransom. When
the expedition fought and captured the Spanish ship *Havre de Grace* in
the Gulf of Guayaquil on 15 April, Hatley was in *Duchess*'s pinnace as
part of a planned boarding party. And when the main part of the expedition moved to capture Guayaquil on 18 April, Hatley was among those
left behind to guard the Spanish prisoners.

With water becoming short, Hatley and another officer were detailed

Guayaquil

to take two of the captured ships and go to Puna Island to collect water and seek news of the expedition. There they met Rogers and learned that the attack on Guayaquil had been successful, although not as profitable as had originally been hoped.

Rogers set off to circumnavigate the globe, but Hatley remained in command of his captured barque. Many sailors fell ill from a disease contracted in Guayaquil, and the search for fresh water became increasingly desperate. When Hatley's ship went astray, Rogers turned back and made frantic attempts to find him. Lanterns were hung and guns fired. Hatley had perhaps six sailors under him, and about the same number of prisoners. It was assumed that the prisoners must have murdered the crew. Wrote Rogers in his account of the expedition, "We all bewailed Mr Hatley and were afraid he was lost."

Food was also running out—one prisoner starved to death—so Hatley was forced by his crew to make for the coast of what is now Ecuador. There, in late May 1709, a native spotted the ship, and Hatley and his crew were captured. The natives abused them, but a priest intervened, probably saving their lives. Hatley and his men were transported south to Lima, now in Peru, where they were confined in the prison on the Plaza Real. Hatley was tortured by the Inquisition, once even being taken to the gallows with a colleague and half-strangled before being cut down. Hatley arranged to smuggle several letters out, but only one survives, dated 6 November 1709, and addressed to the sponsors of the Rogers voyage in Bristol.

Under the deft persuasion of the Inquisition, Hatley accepted conversion to Catholicism in 1710 and was freed in December, though required to remain in Peru. The merchant sponsors of the Rogers expedition petitioned the British government and in 1711 Lord Dartmouth instructed the new governor of Jamaica to do what he could for British prisoners in the hands of the Spanish.

In 1713, with peace between Spain and Britain restored, Hatley was

Even the horrors of the Inquisition did not persuade Hatley to stay in tranquil Woodstock

allowed to leave and returned to his native land, having picked up the Spanish language along the way. The Rogers expedition had returned in 1711 and the sale of the goods was still ongoing, as was litigation. Hatley was paid £180 10s 2d in August 1713, and later that year an additional forty pounds for his role in the taking of *Havre de Grace*.

Back in Woodstock, Symon Hatley senior had died while his son was away, leaving three rental properties in Woodstock to Simon, though with a life estate to his own widow, giving her the income from the properties for her lifetime. In 1718, mother and son sold the properties for £140.

The War of the Quadruple Alliance (1717–1720) brought a renewal of hostilities between Britain and Spain, so Hatley joined another privateering expedition as second captain of *Speedwell* under expedition leader George Shelvocke. *Speedwell* was the smaller of the two ships that went on the expedition; the larger was *Success*.

Delayed by difficulties over their privateering commissions and a lack of favourable winds, the expedition finally left Plymouth on 13 February

1719. The ships became separated and sailed independently after that; Shelvocke's conduct in doing so was subsequently the cause of litigation.

On 4 June at Cape Frio in Brazil, *Speedwell* encountered a Portuguese ship. In spite of the fact that the Portuguese were allies of Britain, Shelvocke sent Hatley across with an armed crew. They returned with gold and other valuables.

In his journal entry for 1 October 1719, Shelvocke recorded the incident for which Hatley joined his former shipmate Selkirk in being immortalised in literature. The shooting of the black albatross took place about four hundred miles south of Cape Horn and, according to Shelvocke's account, Hatley shot the bird believing it portended ill-luck, and in the hope of fairer winds. (At that time there was no taboo against killing albatrosses; this was something invented by Coleridge when he wrote of the incident.) The winds did not calm, but the ship was able to round Cape Horn, battling northward along the coast of Chile, through stormy weather.

Once clear of the weather, *Speedwell* began raiding along the coast, capturing several small vessels, and Hatley was placed in command of one renamed *Mercury*. At Hatley's suggestion, since he knew the coast, Shelvocke had him operate independently to capture small vessels near the coast of Peru and Ecuador. On 9 March 1720, *Mercury's* crew saw a ship that they initially assumed to be *Speedwell*. When they realised it was a Spanish warship, *Brilliant*, it was too late to make a run for it.

Hatley sent sailors who looked obviously British below, trying to make it appear that his ship was still under Spanish control. Three sailors, British by their dress, suddenly emerged from below decks, and the stratagem failed. *Brilliant* fired, slightly wounding Hatley. The British sailors, including Hatley, were captured and landed at Paita, and transported six hundred miles to Lima.

By this time Britain and Spain were again at peace, and all the prisoners except Hatley were soon released; he was kept chained and in soli-

Doré's *"I Watched the Water Snakes"* from the first edition of *"The Ancient Mariner"*

tary confinement. He was accused of piracy because of the looting of the Portuguese ship at Cape Frio, and he faced hanging or hard labour in the mines. There was uncertainty as to whether the Lima authorities could try him for a crime against the Portuguese, and with Shelvocke's reputation already poor even among the British, they decided the expedition commander was probably responsible. Hatley was released in 1723.

Port Royal, Jamaica: many former privateers turned to pure piracy and holed up here

What became of Hatley after that is uncertain. He faced the possibility of a piracy prosecution in England because of the Cape Frio incident. Immediately upon his return to England, he sailed for Jamaica, then a safe haven for pirates, without presenting himself to the owners of the Shelvocke expedition for his share of the loot. Nothing is known of him thereafter.

3

The fortunate cooper

IN THE AUTUMN of 1767 Ann Alder of the Mitre public house in Stert Street, Abingdon, handed her husband John twenty-two pounds to pay the brewer's bill. Evidently Mrs Alder held the purse strings, and her husband's subsequent actions reveal why. Unknown to Ann, John kept back twelve pounds and popped in to the Crown and Thistle on Bridge Street to buy a ticket for the state lottery for £12 18s 6d—around two thousand pounds today. As well as being a cooper and a landlord, John Alder was one of those gamblers who refused to be disabused of the idea that they will strike it lucky with their very next bet.

State lotteries were established in the 1690s by the Bank of England to generate money for "good causes"— to build infrastructure such as bridges—and also to enable Britain to go to war. The state lot-

Site of the Mitre in Stert Street, Abingdon

Drawing the lottery at Coopers' Hall in London

tery was a remarkable success in the eighteenth century, starting with the Queen Anne lotteries of 1710–14. This form of gambling combined the advantages of rational calculation and inexpensive fantasy with quick results. Unlike card games, there were no angry losers. Unlike horse racing, there were no behind-the-scenes expenses or fixing of outcomes. The lottery assured potential punters that they could not lose: they might potentially win a life-changing amount of money, and at the very least they would get back their original stake.

In 1694 the first state lottery, known as the "Million Lottery", was instituted, and formed the pattern on which a further forty-two such lotteries were held. Managers, or directors, were appointed by letters patent to produce books of numbered tickets, mostly costing ten pounds, but in some lotteries costing one guinea, three pounds, five pounds, ten pounds or one hundred pounds. In the ten-pound and hundred-pound ticket lotteries, all purchasers were guaranteed some return, either as a prize or as an annuity, although not the full return of their original stake.

"Fortunate" ticket holders received annuities or prizes in addition. In the lotteries for which tickets cost less than ten pounds, purchasers were not guaranteed any return, and only "fortunate" ticket holders won annuities. The managers printed lists of the winning ticket numbers and the holders' names, and transferred the original lists to the Exchequer. The holders exchanged their own ticket for orders for payment on the Bank of England.

Britain had succumbed to "gambling mania", and large sums were brought in to the Treasury, providing the funding for numerous major wars. As well as individuals, many borough corporations bought lottery tickets for the benefit of poor children; the church was also involved with many parish clerics gambling. Ticket prices were high, but then so were the prizes; this led to people who couldn't afford to buy a full ticket purchasing a share. People placed advertisements in the newspapers to find others to share with, and it was even possible for gamblers to insure themselves against drawing a blank. There was usually one prize-winning ticket for every four blanks.

With two trades, barrel-maker and innkeeper, John Alder would have had a

An eighteenth-century cooper in his workshop

good standard of living. He was in a position to train his own son William as a cooper, thus avoiding the considerable expense of paying a master craftsman to provide a six-year apprenticeship. But even a man who can feed and house his family comfortably might fall prey, if he is that way inclined, to the weakness of frittering away any excess income.

One night in mid-November a messenger in a state of great excitement pulled up outside the Mitre in the London coach. The coach was driven by Francis Blewitt and it also carried James Powell, landlord of the Crown and Thistle where the winning ticket had been purchased. The Alders were in bed and Blewitt had to call up to their window. Alder was told that he had won first prize in the lottery—a sum of twenty thousand pounds, the equivalent of around three million today.

We are told that a bleary-eyed Alder suspected this was a practical joke, suggesting that his weakness for gambling was well known among his friends. Nevertheless he and his wife came downstairs and received the two men. Persuaded that he had, indeed, won this enormous sum of money, Alder was apparently sufficiently overcome to disappear into

The Crown and Thistle (centre right), where the winning ticket was purchased

The "fortunate cooper" shows off his winning lottery ticket

the backyard on his own for a while to recover from the shock. Then he called in all his neighbours for a celebration. A few days later he and the town clerk, John Bowles, set off for London to collect the money.

Once back home in Abingdon, Alder began to display the generosity for which he became famous. He distributed drinks free to all his cus-

Blewitt's stagecoach was painted with the Guild of Coopers' arms

tomers, neighbours and family, and called for a mop to wipe clean the slate in the bar.

He offered to James Powell, landlord of the Crown and Thistle inn where he had bought his winning ticket, the use "without interest" of half the money he had won. The messenger himself and the two schoolboys who drew the winning ticket also benefitted. The church bells rang out in celebration and the ringers were given a drink and a guinea each.

The poor of Abingdon were at this time suffering from bitter weather and high food prices, so from his winnings Alder gave them bread and meat (two "fat oxen") and supplied clothes for all who needed them. He even purchased a new body for the *Abingdon Machine*, the stagecoach belonging to Francis Blewitt which had brought him the astonishing news. On the door of the coach he ordered to be painted the Coopers' Arms and the number of the winning ticket: 3379.

Mrs Alder, however, was unimpressed by this largesse. Not only had her husband spent on a lottery ticket money which was owed to the brewer, but he would—she felt sure—give away on top of what he had won everything that they already had, finally bringing about the bankruptcy she constantly feared. By March 1768 John was already describing himself on the list of voters for Abingdon as a "gentleman", and so was his son William, suggesting that William must have been aged twenty-one or more by this time.

Then Ann Alder's worst nightmare appeared to be coming true: her husband bought a racehorse. One of the most notorious hobbies known to man upon which to lose money, racing horses was the pastime of lords and land owners, not publicans. But Alder showed his colours as an out-and-out speculator by buying a grey called *Sulphur* from a member of the Fettiplace family.

At this early date, Abingdon races were held on Culham Heath, probably in the field to the north of Thame Lane later bounded by the railway line. *Jackson's Oxford Journal* described the course as follows: "The course is most judiciously laid out, both as a piece of fine racing ground, and also for affording diversion for the company, as the horses may be seen quite round from an easy eminence, without moving from the spot."

Sulphur was entered for the Gentlemen's Fifty Pound Subscription Purse at Abingdon races in September 1768, and won by half a neck. It was so unusual in those days for any ordinary person to own a winning

Abingdon races were held on Culham Heath

racehorse that the bells were rung to mark the occasion. Alder renamed his horse *Prize*.

The man who remained steadfast in his belief that gambling could pay off if only you had the nerve to stick to it became a burgess of the town and a warden of the church of St Nicholas. He presented the church with a set of chimes which rang out at three, six, nine and twelve o'clock until the mid-1850s. John Alder died in 1780, by which time he was over sixty. In due course, his son William Alder became a governor of Christ's Hospital and three times mayor of Abingdon. In 1816 he wrote his will, dividing the family fortune between his three sons, John, William, and Charles, and leaving a legacy to Christ's Hospital.

Up until 1810 the local corporation supported Abingdon races, but when their support wavered the races transferred to Abingdon Common (roughly where Tesco now stands). Within a year racing flourished once again. The inaugural meeting on the new course took place in September 1811, and racing continued there for seventy-five years until 1875.

With the defeat of Napoleon in 1815, Britain entered a century of peace, and lotteries were no longer necessary to finance wars. Government lotteries were abolished in 1826.

Long Alley almshouses, Abingdon, by Harry Goodwin (1842–1925)

4

The mock candidate

SEVERAL MEN NAMED "William Castle" lived around Banbury in the late-eighteenth century, but the one wearing a lady's curly wig and bonnet was presumably fairly easy to spot. This particular William Castle, dubbed "Old Mettle" on account of his sometime occupation as a collector of scrap metal, might today be described as "differently-abled", with his very bent leg, pronounced limp, and gaping mouth. He survived by splitting wood into matches and dipping the ends in brimstone. He walked the streets carrying a bundle of them on the end of a stick over his shoulder, and sold a penny-worth or halfpenny-worth at a time. He was a born comedian, full of oddities of speech and drollery.

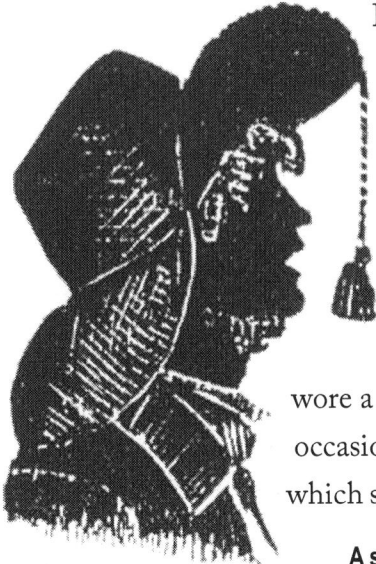

Born to John and Ann Castle in Adderbury in 1793, Old Mettle lived by his wits, and a suspicion that he was more knave than fool prompted somebody to give him a college cap and gown to add to his eccentric wardrobe. His favourite dress was of the oddest patchwork that he could put together. Sometimes he wore a huge cocked hat like a beadle, on another occasion a straw bonnet of enormous dimension which some English lady had brought from Paris.

A silhouette of William Castle, or "Old Mettle"

Although his father John is listed as a weaver on William's baptismal record, Mettle himself was said to have lived among canal boatmen. In early childhood his leg was supposedly caught between the tow ropes of two passing barges and so severely lacerated that he was lamed for life. He would limp from village-wake to village-wake, where he amused the gaping crowds around him by playing the fool. For years most people took it for granted that he really was a fool, and one day somebody helpfully informed Mettle accordingly. Mettle clarified promptly that, while there was indeed always one fool in every family, in his case it was his brother because his brother went to work and he did not. Old Mettle was evidently pretty quick-witted, but at the same time he knew which side his bread was buttered.

He is remembered as the Fool of the Adderbury, Bloxham and King's Sutton Morris set, and this provides a possible clue to his eccentric daily existence. This troupe always came to Banbury for a few days at Whitsuntide when Old Mettle, in fancy dress, brandishing his staff with its bladder and calf's tail, would keep the crowd at a distance whilst his ready wit, grimaces, and powers of contortion kept people in roars of

The Fool would swing a stick with a pig's bladder tied to the end

laughter. One side of his face might be shaved and the other not, or one side painted black and the other white—a device still popular today. Part of the Fool's role was as receiver of donations, so perhaps William saw no reason why he should not stay permanently in character and collect alms from those around him for his daily sustenance.

Having frequently rested overnight on people's door-steps, he would be up early in the morning to go on his rounds. People would give him food from their pantries, and he would beg tobacco from the grocer's shop in Parsons Street in Banbury. When the boys teased him, he would swing round his rod with its line and tail at the end and connect it with their backs with such a whack that it made them squeal. Hence his name was used to terrorise recalcitrant children, to whom he was known as "the Bogeyman".

In fact, this characterisation was very wide of the mark. On public occasions such as fairs Mettle was known to guard the children of poor people who, unable to avail themselves of domestic help, were obliged to take their brood with them wherever they went. He would demonstrate great concern for these urchins, laying the quiet ones gently down, and taking up each squalling one in turn, dandling it like a parent. Far from expecting payment for this service, frequently Castle would bestow his last a halfpenny

A commercially-produced lithograph based on a painting in Banbury Museum

Banbury Green and Horse Fair, occasional scene of Old Mettle's child-minding service

upon the wretched parents. A singular appearance and startling habits evidently masked from the superficial onlooker his genuinely kind and brave qualities. Sadly, though, his character was not without stain.

Castle's criminal career appears to have depended upon householders being absent at work during the day. Perhaps he was such a common sight in Neithrop that nobody questioned the matter when he was seen loitering around the house of John Currell early in 1823. Three one-pound notes proved too tempting, and they disappeared inside William's dubious clothing. According to the *Oxford University, City, and County Herald* of 12 June 1841: "He was tried at Oxford on a charge of being concerned, with others, in a burglary at Neithrop: he tried playing the fool in Court, in order to get off, and made most ugly faces at the Judge; but it wouldn't do there—he was found guilty, and sentenced to be hanged, at which Mettle grinned worse than before. But here fortune favoured him at last, for a petition from his Banbury friends shewed him to be generally considered an idiot, and then he received a pardon."

When smallpox raged through the town between June and September 1827, dog-whipper Thomas Briner felt he was getting too old to dig graves. (He died in 1839 aged 68.) He certainly had plenty to do; his office also included attending to the chiming of the bells, winding up the clock, attending generally to the churchyard, and lighting fires to warm the church for services. Mettle's obituary in the *Oxford University, City, and County Herald* states that he soon became "the constant and fearless nightly burier of the dead."

According to a witness quoted in *Shoemaker's Window: Recollections of a Midland Town before the Railway Age*: "I will endeavour to describe the fair which took place when that dreadful calamity fell upon the town, and the small-pox came upon us. It was at a Twelfth Fair [held in January and sometimes a horse fair]. This was a large affair at this time, as was the Michaelmas Fair, but was a pleasure fair entirely, and there were a lot of shows and other amusements. In one of these shows was a *camera obscura*; this was quite a new sight at fairs and obtained a large amount of patronage. But in another part of this same show was a man dead with the small-pox, unknown to the people who visited it, and this was how so many caught the disease, not only in the town but in the neighbourhood."

Mettle's generosity was further evidenced by his willingness to be not only the author but also the butt of bawdy humour when, at elections between 1818 and 1831, he allowed the townsfolk of Banbury to propose him as the candidate in opposition to the "Guildford interest" (that is, any candidate supported by the local magnate, Lord North).

Recalled the *Banbury Guardian* on 5 June 1841: "Poor Mettle used to climb upon the town hall steps, and harangue the gaping multitude after this fashion: 'Gentlemen, you shall none of you do no work when I go to Parliament, and you shall all have a half-peck loaf for fourpence.' The eloquence of Mettle was usually received with unbounded applause; but unfortunately his benevolent views lacked discernment in one particular—for Mettle could never point out the way in which those persons who were to do no work could come by the fourpences to buy their loaves with. Just such a scheme is that of the Whigs and Mr Tancred, for ruining the town and trade of Banbury, and then mocking the people with the offer of cheap, bad bread, which they could find no fourpences to pay for!

"As the scheme of Mettle, and that of the Whigs and Mr Tancred, are thus identical, we submit to the public that, in common justice, Mettle, as being the original inventor, ought to have the credit of it: and though he was formerly but a mock-candidate… we think he ought now [to] be brought forward as a real candidate for Banbury… Besides, there is something in Dean Swift's witty advice concerning his countrymen. 'If,' he says, 'we are to have blockheads, at least give us leave to have our *own* blockheads.' A blockhead, Mettle may be, and very likely is; but, upon the witty dean's own shewing, if Mettle were to contend with Tancred, he ought to win at a canter.'"

This is, of course, typical contemporary political satire. Certainly there would never have been any serious intention of putting Castle up as a candidate for Parliament. Castle's candidacy between 1818 and 1831 would have had many psychological and social aspects. Among the former was legitimate political expression by the disenfranchised which was sanctioned, even encouraged, by the establishment. During this period political rallies and elections often featured bands playing in the streets, parades, dressing-up—even if simply wearing favours made of ribbons—and plenty of free beer. They might also end in a thoroughly enjoyable riot. The death of George III caused another election within two or three months, and by now Mettle's supporters had increased so vastly in numbers (and pugnacity) that a riot did indeed ensue.

According to *Jackson's Oxford Journal* on 18 March 1820: "On Friday the 10th inst, being the day appointed for the election of a Member of Parliament for this borough, a large concourse of people assembled, and it being generally understood that the usual practice of distributing beer and ribbons to the populace was to be discontinued, the persons assembled soon began to shew strong symptoms of disapprobation, by hissing, groaning, &c. and many of them paraded the streets with favours made of deal shavings in their hats. Whilst this was going on, a party proceeded to the White Lion Inn, and took possession of an old chaise, in which they placed a poor half-witted fellow, nick-named Mettel [sic], and drew him to the Mayor's house, crying 'Mettle for ever!', 'No Legge!'"

According to Sarah Beesley in her book *My Life*: "It had been intimated that there would not be so much beer given away as formerly, which enraged the mob. The Corporation tried to mend matters by offering beer, but this peace offering they then refused to accept. Bloxham, the sheriff's officer, put his head out of a window holding a jug in his hand, and called out 'Plenty of beer! plenty of beer!' but a shower of stones made him speedily withdraw.

Banbury Town Hall, scene of Old Mettle's political campaigns

"Two men then appeared carrying a large tub of beer slung on a pole; this the mob poured down a drain in the market place. The pebbles with which the market place was paved were turned up and used as missiles, the windows of the town hall being completely smashed. The mob threatened to pull the town hall down with the Corporation inside it, and began picking at the pillars which supported it. The vicar of Banbury, who was a member of the corporate body, climbed into a sort of cock-loft under the clock; this did not bear his weight, and he went through. But happening to bestride a joist, he sat there with his legs dangling through the ceiling. Many others were hurt, and much rioting continued all day and night."

The Reform Bill of 1832 gave Mettle's supporters a meaningful vote and they turned their backs on him, putting an end to the electoral fun. In spite of the Reform of the Poor Law, however, the authorities dared not remove completely the source of such merriment, and Mettle was granted outdoor relief rather than being committed to the workhouse.

Did the end of his career in politics tempt Old Mettle back into crime once more? The records of Banbury gaol show that one William

Banbury South Bar in 1833, by Joseph Scarcebrook (c.1818–1906)

Adderbury from the south-east in 1800, from the *Gentleman's Magazine*

Castle was brought in on 22 August 1830 for stealing a watch. That the crime took place in Neithrop, as did Mettle's first offence, would appear to suggest that the William Castle concerned was the Banbury Fool. However, Mettle had stayed out of trouble since that narrow escape in 1823, and this crime seems to have marked the commencement of criminal spree perpetrated by a gang that included a different and younger William Castle. In the latter's case, it ended in transportation.

The only other misdemeanour which can definitely be laid at Mettle's door is the breaking of Mr Grimbly's windows in April 1835—most likely High Street grocer Richard Grimbly. William was ordered to sit in the stocks for four hours.

Old Mettle's death was sudden. In 1841 he was found dead on the road to Banbury from Adderbury, with his bundle of rush-lights still attached to its stick. On the preceding evening he had, in the vocation of Fool, accompanied a party of Whitsuntide Morris men round Banbury, and seemed in high spirits. On the following morning he got up and began to mend his patchwork outfit in order to go to Adderbury club. He was apparently staying at a lodging-house kept by a Mrs Thorp

St Mary's church, where William Castle was buried in 1841

and, as he sat by the grate, he was also nursing the Thorp baby. Suddenly he said to a little girl who was also in the room: "Take the babby," and promptly slumped against the grate. The frightened girl fetched her mother who sent for the doctor, but before he could arrive Mettle was dead.

Ever since his last fair, when someone tripped him up and he fell heavily backwards, he had complained of pain in his head. It emerged that he had also suffered two fits. The surgeon who made the post mortem examination stated that, on opening the head, he found that death had been caused by an effusion of blood on the brain which had probably been exacerbated by his exertions the previous day. A jury returned a verdict of "Death from apoplexy".

Old Mettle did not allow his unconventional appearance to make him a victim, and he created a role in society by exploiting people's reactions to it. He was buried at St Mary's in Banbury in June 1841. The parish register gives his final residence as Grimsbury and his age as 52.

5
The hungry palaeontologist

"WHAT RULES THE WORLD?" demanded William Buckland, Oxford University palaeontologist and Chair of Zoology, as he dropped the skull of a large hyena into the lap of a startled student during a lecture. When the student was too stunned to answer, Buckland boomed: "The stomach, sir! It's the stomach that rules the world. The great ones eat the less, the less the lesser still..." Therefore, he reasoned, whoever dominates the world of plants and animals can, and should, eat all the others.

William Buckland went his own way, sometimes against contemporary thinking

William Buckland

And to demonstrate this theory, that's exactly what he did. Buckland made it a lifelong project to munch his way through as many as possible of the species collected together in Noah's Ark. William's equally-eccentric son Francis even arranged with London Zoo that he should receive a chunk cut off any deceased resident. William Buckland was born at Axminster in Devon in 1784. As a child, he would accompany his father, the rector of Templeton and Trusham, on his walks collecting fossils, including ammonites, from the Jurassic-era lias rocks exposed in local quarries.

He came up to Corpus Christi College, Oxford, graduated in classics and theology in 1804, and became a fellow of the college. His interest in natural history grew and he began to amass a great collection of rocks and fossils. He also attended lectures by John Kidd on mineralogy and chemistry, developed an interest in geology, and carried out field research on strata during his vacations, preferring to wear his academic gown for the job.

Obtaining his MA in 1808, Buckland became a Fellow of Corpus Christi in 1809. He continued to make frequent geological excursions on horseback to various parts of England, Scotland, Ireland and Wales.

In 1813, Buckland was appointed Reader in mineralogy, giving lively and popular lectures with increasing emphasis on geology and palaeontology. These lectures attracted many senior members of the university such as Darwin's mentor Charles Lyell.

Early in his career, from his investigations of fossil bones at Kirkdale Cave in Yorkshire, he concluded that the cave had actually been inhabited by hyaenas in a time before Noah's Flood, and that the fossils were the remains of these hyaenas and the animals they had eaten, rather than of animals washed from the tropics by the surging waters, as had been thought previously.

But as a man of his time Buckland believed that his purpose was to align the geological evidence with the biblical account of creation, so he explained the thin layer of mud covering the remains of the hyaena den as having been deposited in the subsequent "Universal Deluge". He developed these ideas into his great scientific work *Reliquiæ Diluvianæ, or, Observations on the Organic Remains attesting the Action of a Universal Deluge* which was published in 1823 and became a best-seller.

On 18 January 1823 Buckland walked into Paviland Cave in south Wales, where he discovered a skeleton which he named the "Red Lady of Paviland" because he at first supposed it to be the remains of a local

William Coneybeare's cartoon of Buckland in Kirkdale Cave, Yorkshire, in 1821

prostitute. Although the skeleton was in the same strata as the bones of extinct mammals like mammoth, Buckland for now still shared the prevailing view that no humans had coexisted with any extinct animals. He attributed the skeleton's presence to a grave having been dug down into the older layers in historical times, possibly by the same people who had constructed some nearby pre-Roman fortifications. The skeleton is now known to be male and to date from around thirty-three thousand years ago.

In 1824, Buckland became president of the Geological Society of London. Here he announced that the fossilised bones previously dis-covered in the Taynton limestone formation at Stonesfield quarry in Oxfordshire were those of a giant reptile which he named *Megalosaurus*, or "great lizard". He wrote the first full account of what would later be called a "dinosaur", and thereafter he would bring his lectures to life by imitating the movements of the various types before his bemused students.

An early attempt at an interpretation of *Megalosaurus*

Mary Morland

As a talented naturalist and illustrator, Mary Morland of Sheepstead House near Abingdon was the perfect wife for William. Their honeymoon year was spent touring Europe, with visits to famous geologists and geological sites. Back in England, their home at Christ Church was filled with geological specimens and exotic pets. Mary continued to assist William in his work while having nine children, five of whom survived to adulthood.

When William suddenly awoke one night and announced: "My dear, I believe that *Cheirotherium*'s footsteps are undoubtedly testitudinal," Mary patiently accompanied him downstairs to the kitchen and prepared flour-paste to spread over the kitchen table. William retrieved a surprised tortoise from the garden and, sure enough, the impression of the sleepy creature's foot in the sticky mess on the table proved almost identical to that of the fossil.

Fossil hunter Mary Anning had noticed that stony objects known as "bezoar stones" were often located in the abdominal region of *ichthyosaur* skeletons found at Lyme Regis. She also found that if such stones were broken open they often contained fossilised fish bones and scales, and sometimes bones from small *ichthyosaurs*. These observations by Anning

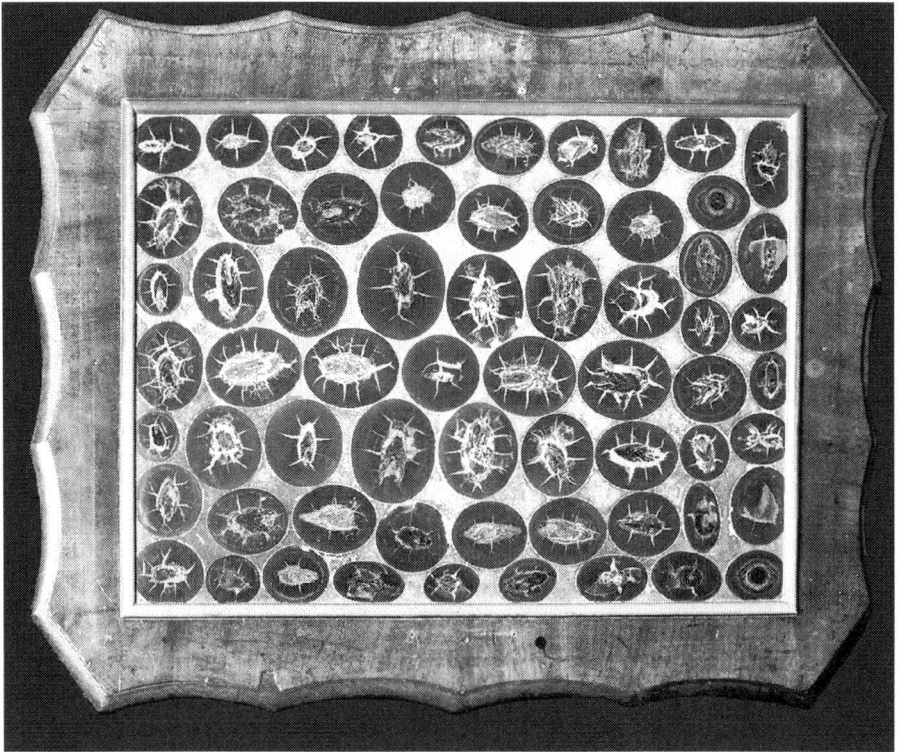

Buckland's table displaying his collection of fossilised dinosaur poo

led Buckland to propose in 1829 that the stones were fossilised faeces. He coined the term "coprolite", and it came to be the general name for all fossilised faeces. He had a table inlaid with a variety of dinosaur coprolites.

Buckland also concluded that the spiral markings on the fossils indicated that *ichthyosaurs* had spiral ridges in their intestines similar to those of modern sharks, and that some of these coprolites were black because the *ichthyosaur* had ingested ink sacs from ancient squid. He wrote a vivid description of the liassic food chain based on these observations, which would inspire Henry de la Beche to paint *Duria Antiquior*, the first pictorial representation of a scene from the distant past.

Following a decade during which geology continued to progress, Buckland publicly and bravely asserted in 1836 that the biblical account of Noah's flood could not be confirmed using geological evidence.

Upon Charles Darwin's return from the *Beagle* voyage that year, Buckland discussed with him the Galapagos land iguanas and marine iguanas. He subsequently recommended Darwin's paper on the role of earthworms in soil formation for publication, praising it as "a new and important theory to explain phenomena of universal occurrence on the surface of the Earth—in fact a new geological power", while rightly rejecting Darwin's suggestion that chalkland could have been formed in a similar way. And by 1840 he was actively promoting the view that what had been interpreted two decades earlier as evidence of the "Universal Deluge" was in fact evidence of glaciation.

In 1845 Buckland was appointed by Sir Robert Peel to the vacant Deanery of Westminster. Soon afterwards, he was inducted to the living of Islip, a preferment attached to the deanery since the reign of Edward the Confessor who was born in the village around 1002. Buckland at first spent the summer months at Islip, and later lived there full-time in retirement.

Henry de la Beche's *Duria Antiquior*, 1830

Buckland's rectory at Islip

During his time in Islip, Buckland contributed to the welfare of the villagers by enhancing educational opportunities and advising on sanitation and hygiene. He did much to improve local agriculture and even bought an experimental farm at Middleton Stoney.

Lunch guests at the rectory in Victorian Islip had every right to feel nervous about what to expect. William Buckland and his family made it their business to eat, in a spirit of scientific enquiry, any animal they happened upon. On offer at the dining table might be anything from mice crisped in batter to panther chops, rhinoceros pie, or elephant trunk. Crocodile steaks were apparently reserved for breakfast. Sliced porpoise head, horse's tongue and kangaroo ham were other delicacies of the house—it seems nothing was off limits. However, William did maintain that roast mole was the most unpleasant thing he had ever eaten, until he tried stewed bluebottles.

In the rectory drawing room after one of these terrifying lunches, guests might encounter the family's pet donkey or a monkey that appeared to enjoy access to all areas in the home. Buckland continued to maintain a menagerie at the rectory, including a bear called Tiglath Pileser (a name used by three Assyrian kings) which roamed around the village, dropping in to the local shop in search of sweets.

One day, Buckland was visiting a friend—some say it was the Archbishop of York, some say the scene was Nuneham Courtenay—who

Meals at the rectory were full of surprises

On the look-out for bears: villagers never knew what might emerge from the rectory

wanted to show off a special family treasure kept inside a silver snuffbox. Buckland peered in, and there, cushioned in the box, was a desiccated morsel of the heart of Louis XIV, rescued from the Abbey of St Denis during the Revolution. "I have eaten many strange things," Buckland declared to his friend, "but I have never eaten the heart of a king." With that, and before anybody could stop him, he popped the sacred chunk of the Sun King into his mouth and promptly swallowed it.

On a visit to a church in Italy, the Bucklands' hosts proudly showed them the stains of the blood of the saint martyred on that very spot, blood which miraculously renewed itself every morning. Kneeling down to lick the supposed-blood, William Buckland announced to his hosts that, no, it was in fact bat urine.

By 1850, Buckland was afflicted with a tubercular infection which had spread to his brain. Greatly disabled, eventually he was committed to the Retreat, an asylum in Clapham. He died in 1856, and was buried in Islip churchyard. His collections are housed at the Oxford University Museum of Natural History, and his fossilised-poo table can be seen in the museum at Lyme Regis.

6
The Banbury pedestrian

DURING THE LATE eighteenth and early-nineteenth centuries, pedestrianism, like horse racing, was a popular spectator sport across Britain. Striding along in the outdoors, generally with only one's own endurance to test, the pastime of covering apparently impossible distances within a given time-period became massively popular with spectators partial to a wager.

Horse racing required expenditure of aristocratic magnitude, whereas by completing an heroic walking feat, a fit working man with comfort-

"Pedestrianism": a sport requiring minimal outlay

Shag weaving: from *"The Weaver's Garland, or, A New School of Christian Patience"*

able boots could win a substantial purse using just the legs his god gave him. The sport of pedestrianism was the perfect choice for the free spirit of the Georgian age.

Oxfordshire's representative in this field was one Thomas Colley. He was born in the hamlet of Wickham on the Bloxham Road from Banbury in November 1773, the son of James Colley and his second wife Isabel. Like many in the villages surrounding Banbury, James Colley worked in the textile industry as a shag weaver.

With the advantage of an established wool market, Banbury was ideally placed as a centre for early textile manufacturing in Oxfordshire. The mid-seventeenth century witnessed a rapid growth in road transport by means of horse-drawn traffic, and Banbury's strategic position on the main route from London to Birmingham made the town the focus of a considerable demand for webs, girths, horse-cloths, wednal for lining horse-collars and tilt cloths or awnings for carts and waggons. The manufacture of shag, later known as "plush", spread rapidly through the Banbury district after 1750.

Much of the weaving at this time was done in cottages; yarn was sent out from the main distributing centre in Banbury to weavers like James Colley. Women were not allowed to weave, but they could be employed in some of the ancillary processes such as warping or spinning. A strict apprentice scheme operated, with each weaver being allowed one apprentice only. In James Colley's case, if that apprenticeship was bestowed on his eldest son, it would not have been Thomas. James had a son from his first marriage, plus two sons older than Thomas with Isabel.

In the early years of the nineteenth century, the Banbury textile industry began to decline and there were many unemployed weavers in the district, but those who had branched out into an alternative trade came into their own. Thomas Colley was one of those, and his alternative trade was that of baker.

Thomas married Sarah Hands of Banbury in 1799. The couple set up home in Neithrop on the outskirts of Banbury, and would eventually have all of their four children baptised at the stunning new church of St Mary in Banbury.

According to *Cake and Cockhorse* (Banbury Historical Society, winter 1966) in

The village baker: relentless toil

1811 there were no more than two hundred and eighty-four houses in the whole of Neithrop parish. By and large, these were the typical ironstone cottages still to be seen in many north Oxfordshire villages, with one or two rooms on the ground floor and an all-over garret set into a high-pitched thatch roof, lit by a small dormer window. As a tradesman working from home, Thomas may have needed a third room, or "backhouse", downstairs to accommodate the tools of the baker's trade—a furnace, dough trough, and moulding boards. Outside would be stacked bundles of gorse ready for use as kindling.

Defective or non-existent drainage facilities coupled with inadequate privy accommodation led to the accumulation in Neithrop's streets of heaps of filth, perhaps the reason for the extraordinarily high pavement in Boxhedge Road which lasted until the 1990s.

A Hook Norton baker of the previous century, Alexander Calcott (1616-1682), left in his will furniture and household belongings that suggest a comfortable lifestyle. In a two-storey, six-roomed Hook Norton house domestic cooking was done in the hall, whilst the kitchen became the bakehouse, with a furnace, dough troughs, and moulding boards. In the stable-cum-fuelhouse were five hundred bundles of furze, fuel for baking. The showpiece of the house was obviously the chamber over the parlour, its contents worth more than any other room and showing the level of comfort attainable in a village home by the second half of the seventeenth century. There was a feather bed with scarlet curtains and counterpane, a red rug, a table and eight red leather chairs, four pictures, and fire irons. In exchange for relentless, round-the-clock hard work, Thomas could expect a life of moderate prosperity

The comfortable home of a Hook Norton baker, visualised by R C Coltman

that would enable him to provide a roof over all the Colley heads and to put food on the table before them.

But, like drainage, shopping facilities were sparse in Neithrop. Banbury was a better prospect, so Thomas and Sarah made the move to town. In 1813, by the time of the baptism of Thomas and Sarah's fourth child, Thomas junior, the family had established their business in Bridge Street which runs from the Cherwell up to the medieval market place. New ironstone buildings, probably commercial in nature, sprang up along Bridge Street in the seventeenth century, so perhaps Thomas even enjoyed a smart shop-front.

Any sensible person in the early-nineteenth century would be grateful for such an assurance of warmth and security, and likely prayed for the continued good health necessary to keep the plates spinning. But it would be understandable if, during those long hours of toil, this somewhat uninspiring vision of the future might cause the imagination of a free spirit to wander. What could a man of limited means do to boost his income, and perhaps ease off a bit at nearly forty years old?

The interior of an elegant Regency-era baker's shop

On 10 February 1816, the following announcement appeared in the *Oxford University and City Herald*:

> *"A Challenge for 100 Guineas. I, Thomas Colley, Baker, Bridge-street, Banbury, do hereby make known that I will undertake to go 1020 Miles in Twenty successive Days, for 100 Guineas. To start any time within One Month, from some convenient piece of Ground in or near Banbury.*
>
> *"Banbury, Feb. 6, 1816."*

The first notable exponent of long-distance walking is generally considered to be Foster Powell who, in 1773, walked four hundred miles from London to York and back, and in 1788 walked one hundred miles in twenty-one hours and thirty-five minutes. Another gentleman pedestrian was Captain Robert Barclay Allardice, "The Celebrated Pedestrian" of Stonehaven. His most impressive feat was to walk one mile every hour for a thousand hours between 1 June and 12 July 1809. The feat captured the public's imagination and around ten thousand people came to watch.

Working-class pedestrians replaced the gentry as the main practitioners and began to attract mass audiences. George Wilson, a wiry fifty-year old itinerant pedlar from Newcastle-on-Tyne attempted, in September 1815, to walk a thousand miles at fifty miles a day on Blackheath to the south-east of London. Commencing at the Hare and Billet inn, the proceedings provoked scenes of uncontrolled rowdiness.

When Wilson had to be protected from over-enthusiastic supporters by minders with staves and horse whips, the authorities feared civil disorder and stopped his walk after seven hundred and fifty miles. Wilson was arrested with five days still in hand, and public sympathy resulted in a collection on the Stock Exchange for his benefit to the sum of one hundred pounds.

The publicity around Wilson's adventures on the heath and in the courts appears to have sparked Thomas Colley's ambition to go one better by walking one thousand *and twenty miles* in twenty successive days—one mile a day more than the famous Blackheath Pedestrian.

George Wilson, "The Blackheath Pedestrian"

Following his newspaper announcement, betting on Colley's event was said to be brisk. The wager necessitated thirty-nine-year-old, five foot five-and-a-half-inches tall Colley commencing at five or six in the morning every day and walking around fifty-one miles, which would take him until around eleven at night. In addition to his measured distance per day, Colley of course had also to walk the round trip to his home in Bridge Street.

One wonders what his wife Sarah thought about all this. Did it fall to her, with a three-year-old child still at home, to keep the bakery going for three weeks? Was there an apprentice to help, or a baker's boy to make deliveries? In any event, at dawn on 20 March 1816, Thomas made a start. The quarter-mile course lay in a field alongside the Bloxham Road as it passed through Neithrop.

He put twenty miles behind him before stopping for breakfast, and then another thirty-one before dinner. With a good start under his belt, Colley retired at a civilised half-past eight in the evening.

The next few days were wet and the course slippery. In such miserable conditions, the drum and fife parade along the course must have lifted the spirits. On the first Sunday there was a respectful pause during divine service. After this, a rhythm set in of fifty-plus miles each day, with Colley dropping below his target on only one day.

On the final day, Wednesday 3 April, Colley was accompanied during daylight hours by a young man named James Golby. Possibly the son of Edward Golby of Neithrop, a bookbinder, James was short in stature and a mere twenty-four years old. For what *Jackson's Oxford Journal* called a "trifling wager", Golby completed almost eighty miles well inside his allotted twenty-four hours.

As for Thomas Colley, a three o'clock start and a target of only forty miles ensured that the spectacle reached its climax at seven o'clock in the evening, in good time for all to witness his triumph before retiring to bed. Thomas even completed an extra mile before being carried in a chair up and down the course amidst the acclamations and congratulations of thousands of spectators. Having enjoyed his share of an ox which had been roasting next to the course all day, he went home to Bridge Street to rest.

Next day he was driven round Banbury in a chaise and four, and then "chaired in triumph, attended with many flags, and a large concourse of spectators," according to *Jackson's Oxford Journal*. A subscription was started up in his favour.

But Thomas Colley did not enjoy the proceeds of his project for long. He died three years later at the age of forty-two and was buried at the new church of St Mary in Banbury on 27 November 1818. So we will never know whether his free spiritedness was a passing phenomenon, or whether he would have gone on to other challenges. Colley's early death left his widow alone to bring up the couple's youngest son, Thomas, who was only five when his father died. Tragically, the boy died in 1828 at the age of sixteen. Sarah's first two sons, William and Thomas, appear only in baptismal records, and may have died early too.

By 1841, Sarah Colley was living alone in Broad Street, Banbury on "independent means", perhaps savings or an annuity—possibly even the proceeds from the fund raised as a result of her husband's feat of endur-

Thomas was driven round Banbury in a chaise and four

The new church of St Mary in Banbury, burial place of Thomas Colley and his wife

ance walking. Whatever were their source, Sarah's means did not last, and she found herself in a tricky position by the 1850s.

Still alive at the time of the walking challenge was Thomas and Sarah's daughter Ann who married book-binder William Willis in 1831. By 1851 the Willises were living with their five children in Upper Church Street in Neithrop, and Ann was supplementing the family's income by working as a bonnet maker. But in the 1861 census there was no sign of William Willis, and Ann was running a shop and taking in lodgers.

Even if her daughter Ann had been in a position to take her in, though, Sarah may have preferred her independence. Unlike the shame associated with the workhouse, the grant to a respectable widow of a place in an almshouse conveyed an air of modest pride. Only the blameless qualified for the honour.

Sarah Colley's death at the almshouses in Church Lane in Banbury at the age of eighty-eight was announced in the *Oxford Chronicle* as having taken place on 17 December 1859.

7

The body-snatcher of Bodicote

BUSINESS WAS BRISK at the sign of the Red Lion in Banbury on the morning of 20 October 1831. Banbury Fair was in full swing, and joint-landlords John and Edward Churchill looked forward to one of their best days of the year.

Customers spilled out into the yard of the medieval coaching inn, and serving girls dashed to and fro with trays of frothing ale. But after a while, the happy atmosphere was sullied by a strong and nauseating

The courtyard of the Red Lion, with Banbury High Street seen through the archway

The front of the Red Lion (left) before it was replaced by F W Woolworth in 1931

smell. When the customers could bear the stench no longer the search was on, and the source was eventually tracked down to the cart of Joseph Tyrrell, a thirty-five-year-old agricultural labourer from Bodicote. The box on the back of Tyrrell's cart was opened and, to everyone's horror, inside was the corpse of a young girl.

Twelve-year-old Mary Ann Roberts from Broughton had been at the fair on the previous Thursday, then died suddenly on Sunday. On 18 October, she was buried in the lonely churchyard at Broughton Castle, but her body was soon disinterred under cover of darkness by a gang of body-snatchers planning to sell her corpse for dissection. Perhaps understandably after the ghastly activities of the night, in the morning the gang's driver, Tyrrell, had stopped off at the Red Lion for a stiffener on his way to despatch the goods via the Union Coach to the buyer in London—probably one of the medical schools.

The nineteenth century ushered in a new-found medical interest in detailed anatomy thanks to an increase in the importance of surgery. Human cadavers were needed, but the Murder Act of 1752 stipulated that only the corpses of executed murderers could be used for dissection. By the early-nineteenth century, public scruples led to a reduction in the number of executions, and consequently the demand for bodies began to outstrip supply. For enterprising sorts like Joseph Tyrrell, the attack of conscience afflicting the middle classes over the death penalty presented a lucrative business opportunity: body-snatching. The season ran from October to May, covering the period during which anatomy was taught in the medical schools. A corpse gave off a strong enough odour without the added problem of heat, so dissection usually took place only during the cooler months.

Corpses were priced on a sliding scale depending on age and size. An adult of either sex, generally over three feet in length, would sell for about four guineas—several months' wages for a humble labourer. But the practise could also be difficult and dangerous. "Resurrection Men", as they were sometimes called, had to avoid detection while they dug up the body and then to deliver it before it became too badly decomposed.

The graves of the poor were preferred because they were unlikely to be guarded. Body-snatchers usually worked at night and in teams. They preferred graves that were covered roughly so that their work would

Only the body would be extracted to avoid the charge of grave-robbing

go undetected. Contrary to popular depictions, body snatchers rarely dug up the entire coffin. Instead, they dug a vertical tunnel down to the head-end of the coffin, broke the lid, and hauled the body to the surface with a rope or a long metal hook. The clothes were tossed back into the coffin, the tunnel filled in, and the ground smoothed to make it appear undisturbed. The practice of returning the possessions of the deceased to the coffin created an important distinction between body-snatching and grave-robbing. In the eyes of the law, a dead body was not considered to be real property but grave clothes were, so the theft of such items carried a higher penalty. This nice distinction may have encouraged opportunists like Tyrrell and his gang to exploit an apparently "victimless" crime rising out of the new need of a comfortable professional élite for bodies, by supplying which the poor might supplement subsistence wages.

So at 7.30am on the morning of the 20th, Joseph Tyrrell, a man with a wife and four children, was committed to Banbury gaol in the Market Place. He was charged, according to the deputy keeper's records, with "bringing a box containing a Corpse, to go to London".

Old Banbury gaol in the Market Place was one of the first buildings in Banbury to be rebuilt after the ravages of the Civil War. Between 1654 and 1656 it achieved notoriety as the place where Quakers were imprisoned. One of them described it as: "A close nasty place, several steps below ground, on the side whereof was a sort of common shore that received much of the mud of the town that at times did stink sorely." Towards the end of the seventeenth century the rooms above the gaol were used as the town's Staple Hall for the sale of wool, but in 1705 they were taken over by the Blue Coat Charity School which continued to meet there until it was merged with the newly-founded National School in 1817.

When Tyrrell arrived in 1831, he would have been housed in one of a row of cells overlooking the courtyard within. An old sketch of the gaol shows that there were no windows on to the market place on the

Banbury gaol, still standing today, but much disfigured in the 1960s

ground floor; the only daylight in each cell was provided by a small, barred window onto the courtyard. On the right-hand side of the court-yard, a treadmill had recently been installed.

The next day, Tyrrell was taken before the magistrate and informed that, if he failed to find securities by 2pm on Monday to guarantee that he would not abscond, he would be committed to Oxford gaol. Needless to say Tyrrell, a penniless labourer, failed to find the money. So, at 4am on 25 October, he was put in a coach for Oxford, escorted by the arresting officer Constable Claridge.

Joseph Tyrrell's wife Mary had to wait ten weeks to learn her husband's fate. At the Epiphany Sessions in Oxford on 3 January 1832, Joseph was sentenced to twelve months in the castle gaol, his offence being recorded as "stealing a body from a grave". As we have seen, a body was not considered legally to belong to anyone, but Joseph's fairly stiff sentence foreshadowed the Anatomy Act which would become law in the following July and reflect pubic distaste for Resurrection Men. Even

Rumours have long linked the village of Bodicote with Resurrection Men

so, it must be compared with a sentence handed down to one Daniel Purbrick during the same court session for stealing a deer. An habitual poacher, Purbrick was transported to Tasmania. Tyrrell refused to give up his accomplices, though back in Bodicote the names "Walton" and "Chilton" were whispered. Probably, in return for his loyalty, Joseph's co-conspirators kept an eye on the Tyrrell family while he was absent.

After Joseph's release, things quickly returned to normal in Bodicote. Four more children were born to the Tyrrells, though the first, Mark, born in 1834, went unbaptised; perhaps some residual bad feeling on behalf of the clergy lingered. Joseph lived a long and apparently law-abiding life surrounded by his family, dying aged eighty-five in 1878.

But let's not forget the Roberts family over in Broughton. Five years after the sensational discovery of little Mary Ann's decomposing body, her labourer father James died aged fifty-one. Her mother Sarah was left to support a ten-year-old son and five-year-old twins. She disappears from the local census records after 1841.

8

The gypsy who built herself a house

A BEAUTIFUL GYPSY GIRL sashayed through the crowd at Warwick races in the summer of 1816, a stylish beaver-hat perched on her dark curls, and a basket of trinkets balanced on her hip. Tall and slender, with dark hair and hazel eyes, the bewitching Sinetta Smith was fifteen or sixteen years old. She claimed to have been born in Italy.

Also at the races that day was James Lambourne, a twenty-two-year-old horse dealer from Cumnor. He, too, was said to have gypsy blood in his veins, hence his nickname "Gyp Lambourne". The couple fell instantly in love.

The age of consent at marriage during the Regency period was twelve

Warwick races: a mostly-masculine environment, except for gypsy women

"Cartomancing" by **Ludmila Gornichenko: gypsy women had to be strong and capable**

for girls and fourteen for boys, but parental consent to marry by licence was needed for minors under the age of twenty-one. Perhaps because of James's rumoured traveller connections, Sinetta's mother Prettymaid Smith evidently made no objection and the marriage took place at Shipston-on-Stour that same autumn.

At first James and Sinetta took a gypsy caravan (a "vardo") as their home, travelling the countryside and making their living from horse dealing at fairs. They maintained links with the Lambourne family at Cumnor, returning there to over-winter and for Sinetta to have her first two children, a girl baptised Sinetta in 1817 and a boy, James, in 1819.

The Lambourne caravan must have frequently clip-clopped up and down the rough track that was the Banbury Road linking the north of Oxfordshire with the south, or out through Botley and down the hill

The interior of a gypsy caravan, or "vardo"

to Cumnor. When, in 1820, a plot of land by the Banbury Road was offered for sale by a local farmer, the Lambournes snapped it up and decided to make it their settled home.

By happy accident another early resident, John Badcock, recorded the very first days of Summertown. An immediate neighbour of the Lambournes, he described the dynamic couple first-hand, including Sinetta's determination to further their plans single-handed. In the autumn of 1820, while James was away horse

James Lambourne's home village of Cumnor

Cumnor.

The house just out of sight on the right was the Lambourne home, now demolished

dealing, she remained on site in the family caravan collecting stone and materials with her own hands to build a house.

Later, when other houses were built nearby, James instructed St Aldate's painter Costar (probably Benjamin Costar) to paint for him, at a cost of 4s 6d, a board announcing: "James Lambourne, horse dealer, Somers Town". James often told Badcock that his meaning was to name his plot after that delightful season of the year on account of its being in his eyes the "pleasantest place in all England". So James's sign board gave the village the name Summertown which it still bears today.

It is Badcock who gives us the physical description of the beautiful Sinetta, as well as intelligence on her supposed "good temper". James he describes as a "tight, firm-built, active man, five feet four inches tall, and round as a baker's rolling pin who, with his wife, three children, and their man Boss, comprise the household". James and Sinetta were evidently sufficiently well-off to employ a servant.

The Lambourne home was at first a modest cottage, "encircled with a barrier of long upright faggots, fixed close together, as an additional shelter from the inclemency of the weather". After a few years James was able to add a brick-and-sash front to his premises. The house no longer

The young blades of the University would have provided plenty of custom for James

exists, but it stood immediately south of what is now the Dew Drop Inn. On its other side was the King's Arms, according to Badcock a "respectable" brick-built inn with bow windows.

Badcock described the Lambournes themselves as a middle-aged couple with three children. "Lambourne is a horse dealer," he confirms. "His family attend church regularly, but he is seldom there himself." Furthermore, James swore too much and broke the Sabbath, a fault apparently "too common with many in his line of life", that is, gypsies. Sobriety was the greatest compliment the tee-total Badcock could pay to anyone, and James Lambourne was a "sober, moderate man in drinking".

Sober he may have been, but James was not above claiming to be a descendant of the fictional character Mike Lambourne in Walter Scott's smash-hit historical romance *Kenilworth*, published in 1821. It must be said that Scott cleverly weaves truth with fiction so that when, in the very first chapter, one "Michael Lambourne" is welcomed back from abroad to the Bonny Black Bear inn at Cumnor (where there is indeed an inn named the Bear and Ragged Staff), the local Lambourne clan might

well be forgiven for believing that the learned author had uncovered something about their family that they themselves never knew before.

Horse dealing among gypsies has been known to lead to the occasional outbreak of fisticuffs, and James became involved in just such an incident in November 1826. "Wednesday last a pitched battle was fought on Port Meadow," reported *Jackson's Oxford Journal*, "between James Lambourne (better known in this neighbourhood by the appellation of Gyp Lambourne) and James Margetts, a horse dealer; the latter was considerably the heaviest man of the two, but the gypsy proved himself the best; they fought for about half an hour, when Margetts was so much beaten that he could fight no longer, and Lambourne was declared the victor."

Now a man of property, at the beginning of July 1834 James signed his will at the age of fifty. And a few days later, the couple's final child, Esau, was baptised at the newly-built church of St John in Summertown. It seems perfectly reasonable for a man described by his neighbour John Badcock as "increasing in wealth" and with a wife and four children to set his affairs in order. But was there more to it than that? Within a few years, James would be committed to an asylum; was some kind of infirmity already becoming evident?

As well as the Lambourne family home, James's will reveals that he owned a field in Summertown, presumably for grazing horses, plus another next to the workhouse which he used as a "garden", that is, for cultivation. In the village of Wootton, just up the hill from Cumnor, James owned the lease on two cottages which were let at the time to the Widow Bennet. Two livery-stable keepers were appointed executors of the will alongside Sinetta.

One incident suggests that Sinetta was pretty well in charge hereafter. In 1836 a young lad named John Light had been in the service of the Lambournes for only a month when he suddenly disappeared from the house, along with three watches, two gold seals, and a gold chain, value of ten pounds. A report was received that Light had been spotted on the road to Cheltenham. Sinetta set off by coach in pursuit of the thief. She made lightning visits to Cheltenham, Gloucester, Bath and Bristol but without success. However, on her return journey, two men mounted on the same horse passed her coach.

"Stop! Thief!" shrieked Sinetta. The two men fled at a gallop. A spirited chase ensued during which Sinetta, too impatient to sit in the coach doing nothing, leapt out and joined the pursuit on foot. Eventually the coach overtook the men. Sinetta arrived shortly after, presumably a lit-

Sinetta initiated a frantic coach chase after a thief

tle winded, and identified the culprit, who was taken into custody. John Light was brought back to Oxford for trial and within weeks he was transported to Tasmania for life. (He made use of his free passage to became a flour-miller in the gold-rush town of Kyneton, where he lived with his wife and fourteen children.)

It was in the year after this incident that James and Sinetta's daughter, another Sinetta, turned the head of a young man who would eventually change her way of life even more dramatically than James had her mother's. The Honourable Charles Cavendish Bentinck, was a nephew of the Duke of Portland, and grandson of the Marquess Wellesley, Governor-General of India, an older brother of the Duke of Wellington.

"Charley" went up to Merton College in 1837 when he was nineteen. Sinetta, whom John Badcock had described in 1832 as "a little sprightly, but sensible well-disposed brunette" was by now also nineteen, and said to be even more ravishing to look upon than her mother. How the couple met is unclear, but young bucks at the university often brought with them their favourite mount, and James Lambourne's closest friends were livery owners. When Charley

The Hon Charles Cavendish Bentinck

reached twenty-one and could wed without the consent of his guardians, he and Sinetta married at St George's, Hanover Square. The groom gave his address as Brook Street, perhaps his club, and Sinetta was living in Southwick Street where her parents now kept a London establishment as well as that at Summertown.

Charley could not remain at Oxford as a married man, so he forbore to inform the university authorities of his change of status. And crucially, he kept his marriage secret from his family. In the meantime, Sinetta began whitening her dusky skin with a cream containing mercury and lead in order to resemble more closely the typical English lady.

In the following June, at 20 Pickering Terrace in Bayswater, Sinetta gave birth to the couple's first child, a son named Charles. The baby lived for a few weeks only.

In January 1841 James Lambourne died of "palsy" in the private asylum at Bethnal Green, aged fifty-seven. Although the asylum had begun life as a mental institution—and one with a shocking reputation, too—it was by this period used as an infirmary.

According to the census taken on 6 June 1841, Sinetta Bentinck was

The Tudor-built asylum at Bethnal Green, now demolished

staying with her uncle and aunt in Cumnor, and using her maiden name of Lambourne. If Charley was at college in Oxford, a heavily-pregnant Sinetta may have wished to be nearby. Or perhaps she was still in London, and her inclusion in Cumnor in the census was cooked up to fool his family and the university authorities. After all, this was the first census to include details of individual households, and there may have been some suspicion as to its possible use.

In any event, Sinetta was back at Pickering Terrace by July, when she gave birth to another little Charles. But the boy died at the family's new home in Hanwell, Middlesex, in March 1842. His grandmother Sinetta Lambourne was by her daughter's side at the death of another child. And in July 1844, the youngest Lambourne child, Esau, also died in Hanwell, aged ten.

Charley Bentinck at last gained his degree in 1845, and had to break the news of his marriage to his uncle the Duke of Portland, who was predictably furious. Charley was obliged to accept a poorer living as a clergyman than he had hoped. Sinetta Bentinck died of a vascular condition at their home in Ampthill in 1850 and, according to a report in the *Gypsy Lore Journal*, her body was "enamelled to the waist". Had the Bentinck babies suffered from poisoning as a result of their mother's obsession with making her skin more fair?

Sinetta Lambourne had been living at 43a Grosvenor Mews, a crowded and down-at-heel area near Grosvenor Square. Why? Something had gone wrong with her finances because in 1849 she was declared bankrupt. By 1851, (the year John Light married), she was alone in London, lodging, interestingly, in the Somers Town home of a carousel gilder. Did she still, after all these years, still feel more comfortable among the people of the travelling world? She moved round in the same area, eventually dying at 87 Euston Road, St Pancras, in January 1871, aged seventy-five. It was a sad end for a gypsy woman who had dared to break with tradition and give up the travelling life.

9

The transported convict

HORSE THEFT WAS CONSIDERED a major property crime during the eighteenth and nineteenth centuries, the equivalent of housebreaking or highway robbery. Those convicted might expect to be hanged.

At about six o'clock on the evening of Saturday 23 February 1828, twenty-four-year-old groom and sometime thief Charles Dell arrived at the Two Brewers in Wargrave Road, Henley. He brought with him a brown gelding which Gibbs the landlord put into the stables. Dell claimed that his master, a horse dealer at Oxford, had instructed him to wait at the inn till he arrived at midday on the Sunday to collect the horse and take it to Abingdon fair.

Horse theft: a hanging offence

The Two Brewers at Henley

Dell was the son of a Reading wheelwright, but there were older brothers better placed to take over the family business. As an errand boy in London, he had been sentenced to transportation for stealing a packet of silk handkerchiefs. He got as far as the prison hulk *Justitia*, but went no further than Deptford, perhaps because he was found to be under 18.

On the Sunday morning, 24th, the landlord's son James Gibbs overheard Dell offer another patron a "ride out" on the horse later that afternoon, presumably with a view to selling it. This did not add up. If Dell's master was arriving at midday to take the horse to Abingdon, how could Dell offer that same horse for a ride in Henley during the afternoon?

James Gibbs, himself landlord of the Angel Inn at Remenham (now the Little Angel), returned to the Two Brewers early on Monday morning before Dell had surfaced. Having told his father not to allow Dell to remove the horse from the stable, Gibbs informed the magistrate, fetched a constable, and detained both prisoner and horse.

That same evening, Uxbridge coach-master William Tollitt received a message explaining that his gelding, missing since the morning of 3 February, may have been found. Tollitt had never seen the horse, so he took his son Joseph with him to Henley the next day to identify it. Joseph later testified: "I am the prosecutor's son, and know this gelding. It was kept in the stables at Hanwell [Middlesex]. I saw it safe on Friday night, the second, about half-past seven o'clock: I drove it down in the coach that night. I went on to Uxbridge, but left the gelding at the King's Arms public house at Hanwell. It was missed afterwards, and I found it at Gibbs's on the Tuesday following, and knew it to be the same."

Asked to explain how the horse came into his possession, Dell claimed: "I was going down to see Mr Tollitt as I was out of service. I stopped just by Hanwellgate… A man came up and asked if I was out of place. I said yes; he said if I would take a horse to Uxbridge he would pay me for it. I said I could not take it down for less than thirty shillings, and he offered to pay me for it… Next morning he gave me another horse, and told me it belonged to a Mr Crab of Oxford, and told me to take it there."

More convincing was the testimony of Tollitt's ostler John Waite: "On Friday night, the second of February, I left this gelding in the stable, at twenty minutes to ten o'clock, with other horses. It was tied up with a halter in the usual way; I locked the stable door. I went there again about

The Angel at Remenham, now the Little Angel

half-past five o'clock in the morning, found the door open, and this gelding gone. There are two doors to the stable; one was bolted inside, and the other locked. The one which I had bolted inside was wide open. There is a window with a slide to it, which was not fastened. A person could get through the window, open the door, and lead the horse out."

Because the theft took place in Middlesex, Dell was tried at the Old Bailey, and on 24 April 1828 he was sentenced to death. Although the punishment of death for stealing horses was not abolished in the United Kingdom until 1832, actual executions for horse theft had been rare to non-existent for fifty years. Dell's sentence was commuted to transportation for twenty-one years. In June, he was moved from Newgate prison in London to the *Leviathan* prison hulk in Portsmouth.

Convicts sentenced to transportation were sent first to hulks—old or unseaworthy ships, generally ex-naval vessels which had been stripped of their masts, rigging and rudders, and instead fitted with prison cells. Moored in rivers and harbours, they were close enough to land for the inmates to be taken ashore to work. Although originally introduced as a temporary measure, the hulks quickly became a cost-efficient, essential and integral part of the British prison system.

Prison hulk

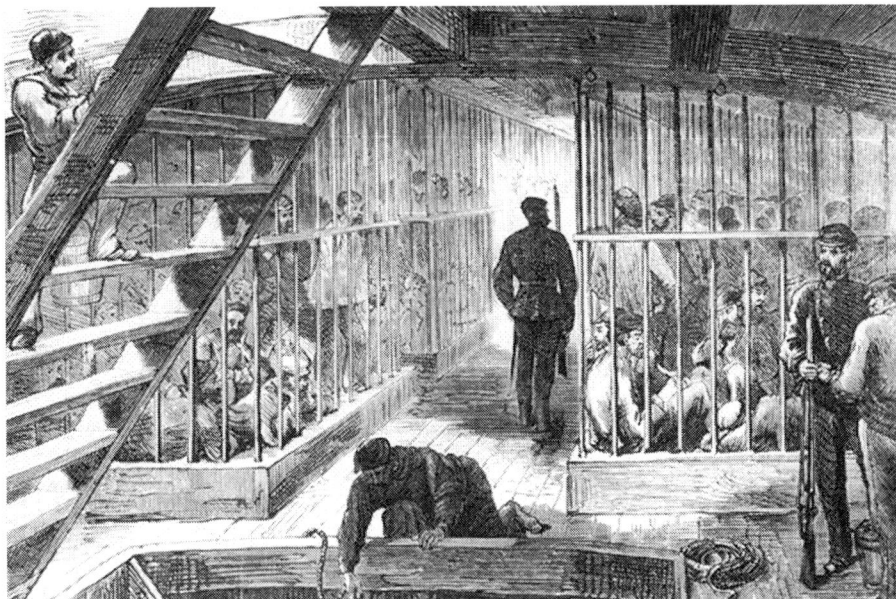

Conditions on board the hulks and transportation ships were appalling

Convicts were washed, inspected and issued with clothing, blankets, mess mugs and plates, and then allocated to a work gang. They spent ten to twelve hours a day working on river-cleaning projects, stone collecting, timber cutting, and embankment and dockyard work while they waited for a convict transport to become available. Typically, each hulk held between two and three hundred convicts in dire conditions. Disease was rife and spread quickly as there was no way to separate the sick from the healthy in the cramped conditions. This meant mortality rates were high, with around one in three inmates dying on board.

After nine months on the hulk, Charles Dell was transferred to the convict ship *Waterloo* which departed for Australia on 12 March 1829, carrying some one hundred and eighty convicts in all. After a sixteen-week voyage, on 9 July the ship arrived at Port Jackson in Sydney.

Only a small percentage of convicts were kept confined; most worked for free settlers, former convicts, or for the authorities. The cost of their board and lodging plus uniform was thus shifted off the government's books. Dell was immediately assigned to the charge of former-convict

Port Jackson in Sydney

Andrew Coss, an Irish-Catholic publican at the Punch Bowl public house in Cambridge Street in the Rocks area of Sydney.

Convicts rarely served their full term and could qualify for a "ticket of leave", "certificate of freedom", "conditional pardon" or even an "absolute pardon". This allowed convicts to earn their own wages and live independently. Convicts sentenced to seven year terms could qualify for a ticket of leave after four years, while those serving fourteen years could expect actually to serve between six to eight years. "Lifers" could qualify for their ticket after ten or twelve years.

When the convicts disembarked, a master in need of labour might take his pick

The Punch Bowl Inn in Cambridge Street, the Rocks, Sydney

Dell's new master Andrew Coss had gained a conditional pardon, giving him the freedom to work and live within the colony until his sentence expired. He was granted fifty acres of land in September 1820. By the 1820s a growing number of freed convicts had been appointed to positions of trust and responsibility and Coss even served on coroners' juries a couple of times.

Coss's establishment, the Punch Bowl, dated from about 1813. It was a long, low, white-washed, rubble-stone house with a gabled roof of shingles. Simple square chimneys at the south end to the rear of the house suggest the taproom and kitchen respectively. The sign outside had the name of the house depicted in pictures—a bowl with two ladles—and hung from a pole at the front.

Employers like Coss did not have to pay their assigned convicts for the work they did, but they did have to provide them with food, clothes and somewhere to live. Some assigned convicts complained to the government about their treatment; others ran away. However, many were well looked after by their masters, and some even stayed on as paid workers once they had finished their sentence.

Charles Dell appears to have moved on from the Punch Bowl because in 1844 he was living on the other side of the Blue Mountains in Bathurst, two hundred kilometres west of Sydney. Why did he fail to apply for his ticket of leave? Had his parents washed their hands of him? Or perhaps, like many transported convicts, he found his life chances were actually better in Australia than back in England.

Bathurst is the oldest inland town in Australia, founded in 1815. It was intended to be the administrative centre of the western plains of New South Wales, where orderly colonial settlement was planned— although the local Wiradjuri people understandably expressed their own views about this by means of open conflict that ended only in the early 1820s. The first licensed inn within the township was opened in 1835, the Highland Laddie. Was it the pub trade that took Charles to this Wild West town?

Justice in Bathurst was tough and summary for convicts. Ralph Entwistle, a Bolton labourer, was convicted of stealing clothing and transported to New South Wales in the year before Charles Dell. After arriving in Sydney, he and a few other convicts were assigned to squatter John Lipscombe and sent across the newly-traversed Blue Mountains to

Bathurst, west of the Blue Mountains

BATHURST.

work on Lipscombe's land near Bathurst. In November 1829, Entwistle and another convict servant drove one of their master's bullock drays to Sydney market to deliver wool and, on the way back, in the fiery heat of the day, the men stopped for a skinny dip in the river.

Governor Ralph Darling and his party happened to pass the naked convicts. The men were hauled before the police magistrate in Bathurst, Thomas Evernden, and charged with "causing an affront to the Governor", despite Darling not having even seen the incident. Entwistle and his companion were each sentenced to a public flogging of fifty lashes.

Within a year, an embittered Entwistle had become a bushranger, taking up armed robbery as a way of life, and using the bush to hide from the authorities. He set about persuading other convicts to join him. The rebels became known as the Ribbon Gang on account of Entwistle wearing "a profusion of white streamers about his head".

In late September 1830, he and his men began raiding farms, seizing firearms and liberating convicts in the process. The gang had grown to fifty by the time they arrived at the farm of Thomas Evernden, seeking revenge. But the magistrate was absent. When the farm's overseer,

Bathurst justice was rough and ready

A bushranger raid on a mail coach

James Greenwood, refused to allow Evernden's convict servants to join the gang, Entwistle shot him dead. As a result, ten men were hanged and their bodies kept on display for a day "as a warning".

Whether Charles Dell had reached Bathurst by 1830 is unclear, but the activities of the Ribbon Gang illustrate the type of society he moved in. He died here in January 1844 aged forty, five years short of finishing his sentence. No other Dells are buried in the cemetery, suggesting that Charles did not marry.

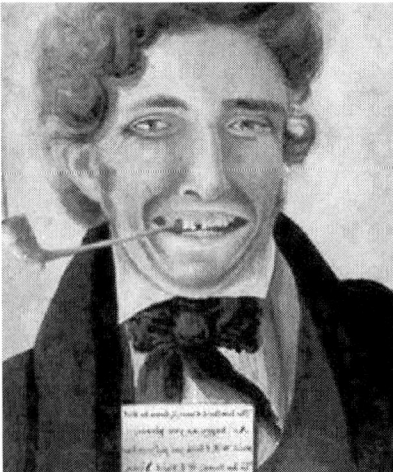

Charles Dell knew the risks when he took Tollitt's gelding. Whether he would have elected to come back to England or not we will never know. Like so many others, he would probably have preferred to remain in a land where work was plentiful and where so many had the last laugh.

The typical idea of an Australian convict

10
The real mad hatter

HOW VERY UNFORTUNATE for a former mayor of Oxford and respected alderman to be summoned before the magistrates. And, worse, that such a figure should be accused of crouching in his shrubbery during Eights Week and shouting orders to the mob on the towpath beyond to kill a humble bargeman and pitch his body in to the river.

Thomas Randall was certainly a colourful character. Son of an Oxford cordwainer, he won a place as a chorister at New College School, remaining there for eight years and benefitting from an unusually fine classical education for the son of a tradesman. Perhaps because of recurring parental financial woes, he would "for a consideration" compose weekly essays for lazy undergraduates to present as their own work.

Owing to the temporary embarrassment of his father's incarceration

Thomas Randall

Randall and his wife Elizabeth Cecil

in a debtors' prison, at the age of seventeen Thomas was obliged to take over his father's High Street boot and shoe manufactory. Having completed an apprenticeship to his father in 1827, he became a freeman of the city. A couple of years later he opened his own shop, the "London Hat Warehouse" at 22 High Street. His life of public service commenced when he became a member of the town council in 1833, and mayor in 1859. The year 1861 was a momentous one for Thomas. It sealed his position as a gentleman, though he generally described himself proudly as a "retired hatter". He was established with his wife Elizabeth and family at Grandpont House, built on an arched stone bridge on the other side of the Thames from the grounds of Christ Church.

Grandpont House in Oxford

Charles Dodgson (Lewis Carroll): a guest at Grandpont House tea parties

A frequent visitor was Henry Liddell, ecclesiastical dean of Christ Church, who would bring with him his daughter Alice. In later life, Alice recounted that she was permitted as a special treat to take Randall's retriever Rover out for a walk. Another member of the circle was Charles Dodgson—Lewis Carroll—who some say took Alice as the inspiration for his heroine in *Alice's Adventures in Wonderland*. It seems distinctly probable that the "Mad Hatter" was based on Thomas Randall himself, a man who gave real-life tea parties in his garden and bore a striking facial resemblance to illustrator's John Tenniel's famous representation of the character.

In July 1861, Randall suffered a severe blow. His son Thomas, who

Thomas Randall and the Mad Hatter: the same man? You decide

Randall's invalid son, Thomas junior

appears to have been sickly for some time, died of "brain fever" at the age of twenty-one. According to *Jackson's Oxford Journal*, in October Randall made a public reference to his personal tragedy rare for a Victorian town dignitary. Accepting the post of alderman, Randall declared that "he felt their kindness the more sensibly at the present moment as they were aware that he had suffered a very heavy affliction in the loss of one whose love and worth had constituted so much of his happiness".

And so to 12 May 1864. Eights Week is a four-day regatta which constitutes the University of Oxford's main intercollegiate rowing event of the year. The races, which provide the background to one of the city's great social occasions, take place in May of each year from the Wednesday to the Saturday of the fifth week of Trinity Term.

Eights Week; the bridge outside Grandpont House is on the left

Randall's guests at Grandpont House that day were John Martin, a doctor, and Frank Spiers, a young man from a family of shopkeepers. The party could watch the fun from their vantage point at Randall's house facing the river. But those who have attended such an event know that any difficulty lies not in gaining access to the event, but in getting out again at the end of the day. At around seven in the evening, the crowd turned its steps towards home.

In full view of Grandpont House, the towpath mounts a narrow bridge across a watery inlet in front of Randall's house. The bridge was, and still is, wide enough only for two people to pass one another safely. As the crowd surged across towards town, bargeman James Edwards attempted to lead his horse over in the opposite direction. An affray broke out during which, claimed Edwards, he was assaulted for no reason. As a result of his allegations, Randall, another tradesman-turned-gentleman Edward Brockliss, and a boatman named Charles Cook were summoned before the magistrates.

Having embarked upon crossing the bridge and seeing no possible resolution, Brockliss attempted to seize hold of Edwards' horse, and

The crowded bridge is pictured here on the right during Eights Week

shouted at Edwards not to go on. The bargeman ignored him and persevered, so Brockliss set about him with his umbrella, claiming in court that he was protecting his wife and child. Even the poor horse received a pummelling, though it is difficult to see where his fault lay.

Several ladies were obliged to climb over the side of the bridge and hung on to the rails from the outside. A mother and her child fell to the ground, and another family became separated in the panic. At this point boatman Charles Cook thrust the pole from his punt through the railings of the bridge and, said Edwards, struck him in the chest several times. Cook countered this, saying he was simply trying to block the path of the horse. Cook's passenger in the punt, Charles Moore—who, happily for the defendants, turned out to be the clerk to the registrar of Oxford County Court—confirmed that Cook intended only to create a barrier in front of the horse with his pole, and called to Edwards, "Go back! Go back!"

Elements among the furious crowd began to push Edwards onto the rails. Randall was about fifteen yards off, and Edwards declared to the magistrates that the alderman encouraged the mob to "throw him in the river and drown him". Edwards' own father backed up his son's account, saying that Randall called out, "Duck him, drown the scoundrel!"

Constable Thomas Kinch, approaching the affray, also heard Randall shout, "Give it him! Duck him!" By now, Edwards had hold of his horse with one hand, and with the other was clutching for dear life to the rail of the bridge. Kinch saw Brockliss beating Edwards with his umbrella, and ordered him to desist, pointing out that he had no right to take the law into his own hands. Kinch heard Randall ordering him to take Edwards into custody, but Kinch saw no offence committed on Edwards' part.

James Blay, a trunk and box maker, was at the foot of the bridge. He saw Cook poking Edwards' body with the punt pole and Brockliss jabbing the bargeman in the face with his umbrella and thrashing the horse.

Scene of the battle (right): a perfectly safe bridge on a normal day

As the terrified horse plunged around in confusion, Edwards fell to the ground, his face streaming blood. Blay cried out to Brockliss, "You will kill the man! Look at his face!" And he heard Thomas Randall chime in, "Serve him right," and that he deserved all he got. Blay felt that, no matter what Edwards had done, he "never saw a man served so brutally".

The matter came to court and, questioned by Randall himself, Blay acceded that he did not hear the alderman incite the mob, though he did hear him say, "Serve him right." Randall happily admitted to this.

Randall then wheeled out his guest on the fateful day, Doctor Martin, who claimed that he was in Randall's house with him throughout, and that his host could not possibly have incited the crowd without his hearing it. Randall's other guest, young Frank Spiers, was even more helpful; he was in the house with Randall, and claimed that his host went out into the garden only to order that Edwards be taken into custody for his own protection. Anyone who said otherwise had perjured themselves.

Magistrate Edward Morland declared that he could not rely on the testimony of a mere constable like Kinch (of *Berkshire* Constabulary, not even Oxfordshire) when it was opposed by "two such clear, reliable witnesses" as Randall's friends. After a case lasting five hours, Brockliss and Cook were fined thirty shillings each, and the case against Randall, mayor of Oxford just six years earlier, was dismissed.

In 1872 Randall and his footbridge before Grandpont House were briefly at the centre of more violence. The new Licensing Act permitted magistrates to reduce licensing hours; consequently in Oxford, as elsewhere, the magistrates were besieged on the one hand by temperance groups and on the other by brewers, publicans and the drinking public. At their first meeting the magistrates could not come to a decision but, largely as a result of Thomas Randall's opposition to alcohol, reduced the hours temporarily to 11pm on weekdays and 10pm on Sundays. Randall also opposed extended hours during St Giles Fair.

On Saturday 7 September, the first evening the new rule applied, an angry crowd gathered at Carfax as soon as the pubs closed and listened to speeches denouncing the town council. Chorusing *Rule Britannia!*, they then made for Grandpont House. Fortunately the house—then as now—was not easy to get to, and a body of police under the command of

Carfax: gathering place for a riot against early closing

Carfax, Oxford.

Protesters threw stones at Randall's house

Inspector Soanes blocked the garden gate from the towpath. Gathering on the footbridge, the crowd began to throw stones at the house. Soanes read the Riot Act from the house and ordered the mob to "clear the bridge, allowing respectable persons to pass". The police then charged the mob and chased them up St Aldate's.

On the following weekend, the authorities were ready for any trouble. Notices of the Riot Act were pasted up around the town, explaining that once it was read aloud, anyone who did not disperse within an hour was guilty of a felony. At ten o'clock in the evening, as a crowd assembled on Carfax, a guard from the Berkshire Constabulary was set up around Grandpont House.

Also at precisely ten o'clock, a message arrived at police headquarters requesting help at a "rick fire" in Holywell. The officers hesitated, suspecting a ruse to draw them away from a potential riot, and they were right. The mob set up their usual chorus of *Rule Britannia!* but, as nobody seemed to wish to take a leadership role and they were thoroughly outnumbered anyway, the protesters dispersed with only a handful of arrests being made.

Apart from this antipathy to drink, however, Randall was no enemy of the working man. One example of this was his instigation of a scheme to provide summer vacation employment at seaside resorts for otherwise redundant (and therefore unpaid) college servants.

At the City Court on Friday 16 September 1887, the Mayor made a statement prior to the commencement of business. He had just received the sad news of the death of Alderman Randall who had passed away at Grandpont House that morning at nine o'clock. His obituary in *Jackson's Oxford Journal* of 24 September 1887 emphasised his generosity to the poorer children of St Aldate's parish—he had provided some of them with a tea-party in the grounds of Grandpont House only a month earlier—and praised a man who "has left a name behind him that will long be affectionately remembered not only in the homes of the rich, but in the cottage homes of the poor".

11

The ghost of Church Hanborough

ONE EVENING IN MAY 1857, elderly shoemaker John Putt was returning home from Bladon to Church Hanborough at about half-past ten. Known to be "quiet and inoffensive", Putt struck off across the field known as the "Sart" (indicating a piece of land converted from forest to arable use) where Farmer Osborn had been kind enough to take the top rail off the stile to enable the public to use the path more easily, just as they had done for the past thirty-eight years.

But even in that enlightened Victorian age, rumours were abroad of a ghost haunting the village, and Putt's eye was therefore naturally drawn in the gloom to a white object under the hedge. He reassured himself that it was just a cow nestling down for the night, but then the apparition began to rise up, growing taller and taller, wider and wider.

Shoemaker John Putt encountered a "ghost"

Osborn Farm at Church Hanborough

As the monstrous thing advanced upon poor Putt, he lashed out with his stick, and was surprised to discover that ectoplasm could be quite resistant. The second blow of Mr Putt's walking stick whisked off a white sheet and revealed none other than forty-one year old local farmer George Osborn.

"You, Mr Putt, have no business here," thundered the ghost.

"And you," retorted the shoemaker, "have no business to act in that way. You ought to be put in the dungeon at Woodstock!"

Osborn grabbed a stick, exclaiming: "I have a stick as well as you!"

"You may use it if you like, as I have used mine," retorted Putt, whereupon Osborn collared the old man, threw him to the ground, and dragged him towards the road, all the while forbidding him the use of the footpath over his field.

George Osborn's sensitivity on the matter of rights over his land at Osborn Farm very likely related to the traumatic events he witnessed as a lad. His father had been imprisoned during the Otmoor Riots of 1829–30 for joining a gang of local farmers who pulled down the banks of the River Ray, flooding the land of Sir Alexander Croke.

Watered by the River Ray, Otmoor was until the early-nineteenth century unenclosed marshland which regularly flooded in winter. An Enclosure Act was passed in 1815 under which a channel was cut between Charlton-on-Otmoor and Oddington, known as the New River Ray, to divert much of the water flow around the northern and southern edge of Otmoor.

When the land was fenced off in 1829, the consequences created an alliance between desperate agricultural labourers, who saw cherished additional sources of income from grazing, wildfowling and trapping disappearing as the wetland dried up, and local farmers who found their own fields inundated when the first drainage attempts led to local flooding.

The people of Otmoor were not prepared to let the major landowners ride roughshod over their interests and drain the wetland. Nocturnal raids disrupted the drainage work and when, following a June deluge of rain, the New River Ray not only overflowed, but threatened to destroy the grass crops of the Otmoor farmers, they cut a breach in the bank and flooded the lands of Sir Alexander Croke instead.

Draining the moor interfered with traditional rights such as wildfowling

Nearly every farmer in Fencot, Murcot, Merton, and Charlton was arrested and taken to Oxford gaol. James Osborn of Merton was among those taken, leaving thirteen-year-old George Osborn at home with his doubtless frightened mother.

Before the magistrates at Oxford town hall, the farmers explained that in view of the threat to their crops, some "speedy and effectual means" had to be taken to get rid of the water. They could not be expected to stand by and watch the income by which they paid their rents destroyed. The magistrates judged this a pretty reasonable argument, and the men were acquitted. The people of Otmoor mistakenly believed that the magistrates' opinion meant that the whole enclosure was null and void and that they could destroy fences with impunity and re-establish the old rights of common. The protest movement gained momentum.

Under cover of darkness, crowds of up to five hundred men with blackened faces ventured on to the moor, frequently disguised as women, and carrying pitch-forks, bill-hooks, and even guns. Whether the Osborn men were among them it is difficult to tell, but this stratagem of disguise would certainly be adopted by George in 1857. Eventually the alliance in the Otmoor villages between labourers and farmers fractured and the authorities regained control. By 1834 resistance evaporated.

In November 1848 it was reported that the Osborns' late barley was standing in about four feet of water. Perhaps such conditions as this, and his father James's death in 1852 were what prompted George's move away from Otmoor. His brother James was already farming in Church Hanborough, but he died in 1853 so this was probably when George took over. He claimed to be innovating new drainage practices "without doing the slightest injury to anyone", presumably a reference to the threatened ruination of his father's land in 1830. But he endured great opposition from those who objected to the sight of farmyard detritus and human excrement streaming on to fresh grassland.

So in 1857, a shaken John Putt tottered in to the Hand and Shears

The Hand and Shears (right): refuge for a bewildered Mr Putt

public house opposite the church in Church Hanborough nursing a badly-bruised arm. Landlord Joseph Laitt asked what had happened to him, and he related the details of his bizarre encounter with Osborn.

A couple of lads, Joseph Hall and Thomas Tuffrey, were in the pub too, and they decided to administer immediate retribution. They went to Osborn's house and pitched stones on to the slates of the roof. When Osborn emerged to see what the noise was about, a stone hit him on the head, knocking off his hat, and leaving a bleeding wound.

In front of a delighted crowd in court at the petty sessions in Woodstock, John Putt brought a complaint of unlawful assault against George Osborn, and Osborn brought a complaint of assault against Hall and Tuffrey. Farmer Osborn was evidently a well-known character locally; Putt's attorney William Brunner announced that, because Osborn "possessed in some degree the gift of speech-making", he would himself take advantage of his right to make a few introductory remarks on behalf of the modest Mr Putt. Brunner evidently intended to enjoy himself.

He began by acknowledging that there was some question over a right of way across Osborn's field but, be that as it may, it did not justify the assault on Mr Putt. As the dramatic tale unfolded in court, there was much laughter at Osborn's expense.

Describing the moment when Putt struck at the "ghost" with his stick, Brunner explained: "After this second blow the sheet was thrown off, and disclosed a something in the shape of a human being—although they could scarcely call him human because it seemed incredible that humanity would descend to such an extraordinary depth of absurdity as so to disfigure itself."

At the point where Osborn and Putt recognised one another, said Brunner: "… the one was terrified by what he had seen and the other, doubtless, was bewildered to think that he had made such a fool of himself." The folk of Woodstock loved it, and when poor Mr Putt added disingenuously that he had not known what the apparition was, and that he did not know of any law against striking a ghost, it finally brought the house down.

George Osborn, naturally, represented himself in court. He said that he had a flock of between seventy and eighty sheep in the field, and that he was bid over fifty shillings apiece for them. On the night before his encounter with John Putt, the sheep had somehow got out and this might have resulted in a great loss to him. He revealed, tellingly, that he suspected certain "young men" of doing the mischief, so he felt entitled to disguise himself to frighten them off for good.

As to the matter of the right of way, Osborn had put up a board declaring: "No road here. All trespassers will be prosecuted," but it had been torn down the next day. Asked why, therefore, he had lowered the rail on the stile to allow easier access to the path, Osborn announced that he thought at that time that there was a right of way, but that now he did not.

The court declared that, until the matter of the right of way was cleared up, they could not deal with the assault. The case was dismissed, and Mr Brunner expressed a hope that, as the former case against Mr Osborn was dismissed, Osborn would show a similarly conciliatory spirit and withdraw his charge against Hall and Tuffrey.

Osborn objected to this and said that the parties were not justified in throwing stones at him, but the Bench strongly urged him to adopt Mr Brunner's recommendation. It was evident, they said, that Osborn had brought the whole thing on himself by his own foolish conduct, and he had been lucky not to encounter a younger man who might have given him a thrashing.

In the end, Osborn reluctantly agreed to withdraw the charge. He left the town hall and, as he made his way along the streets of Woodstock, he was hailed with hisses of: "Ghost! Ghost!"

Difficult George Osborn was now a marked man and, when he found himself in court again a few years later, the lawyers saw an opportunity for some sport. As before, George brought the whole thing on himself by being cussed.

A clause in George's tenancy agreement with the Duke of Marlborough required him once a year to perform, free of charge, one day's team work with two horses and one man for every £50 of rent paid. The Duke's agent asked George to send a cart to transport coals from the railway station to Blenheim Palace. George agreed to send his team of horses and a man, but said that the Duke must provide his own cart.

George was served with a notice of ejectment and, in February 1864,

Woodstock and Blenheim railway station

the matter was explored in court in a spirit of some levity. Did the expression "team work" imply that a tenant must supply a team of horses plus a cart? Or just a team of horses? Lawyers on both sides quoted various snatches of poetry at one another, each seeming to validate their own client's point of view, and there was much merriment in court. Awkward as George Osborn may have been, we might feel a degree of sympathy with him that a matter touching on his very livelihood should be thus trivialised.

No definitive verdict was given on that day, but it looks as if things did not go well for George Osborn. He gave up farming and moved right away, never to play fast-and-loose with authority in Oxfordshire again.

By 1871 he and his wife Elizabeth were established in Rudyard Road in Salford, Manchester. Why he chose the conurbation of Manchester is a mystery. He made his living as an oil merchant, and eventually moved up-market to Cheetham Hill. Elizabeth Osborn died in 1890, and George in the following year.

12

The duelling vicar

THERE CAN'T BE MANY Oxfordshire clergymen who have joined a tribe of aboriginal Australians and fought a duel. Maurice Meyrick showed early signs of free spiritedness when, to the alarm of his parents, he threw up a scholarship at Oxford, and announced that he was off to the other side of the world to make his fortune.

Maurice Meyrick grew up in the village of Ramsbury in Wiltshire. The Meyrick family, originally of Welsh extraction, enjoyed strong links with the clergy and military. Maurice's uncle was the local vicar, and his father taught at the vicarage school, where youths aiming to enter university received a classical education. It was expected that Maurice would make his life within these conventional if unexciting bounds.

All seemed to be going to plan when Maurice won a Bridgman Scholarship to study at Queen's College Oxford. In due course he would be expected to enter the church.

Maurice Meyrick

Meyrick failed to take up is scholarship at Queen's College Oxford

But suddenly he astounded his family by declaring his intention to chase adventure in distant Australia. Perhaps his imagination had been fired by letters from his uncle, Colonel Thomas Meyrick, who had settled in

Port Philip near Melbourne in 1845

New South Wales after retiring from the army. The colonel had written glowing accounts of the prospects offered by a life in the colony, and Maurice felt he wanted to be part of it. He convinced his parents he was in earnest and, with their reluctant support, he set sail.

In the late 1830s Melbourne and its surrounding districts were booming. Settlers were pouring into the area, and prices were skyrocketing. Maurice Meyrick was a young man of twenty years when he arrived at Port Phillip in 1839 after six months at sea. He purchased from the Crown the pastoral licence for the Boniyong run (now Boneo) in the southern part of the Mornington Peninsula.

Maurice had lived in a large family in a close community; now he was out on his own in the middle of nowhere. He made friends with the local aboriginal Australians and was even initiated into their tribe, the Boon Wurrung people of the Kulin nation. The Boon Wurrung travelled in search of food in groups of as many as thirty men, women and children. Before European settlement, this swampy country with its salt-water lagoons, sandy scrubland and dense thickets of tea tree, was rich

The stations on the Mornington Peninsula

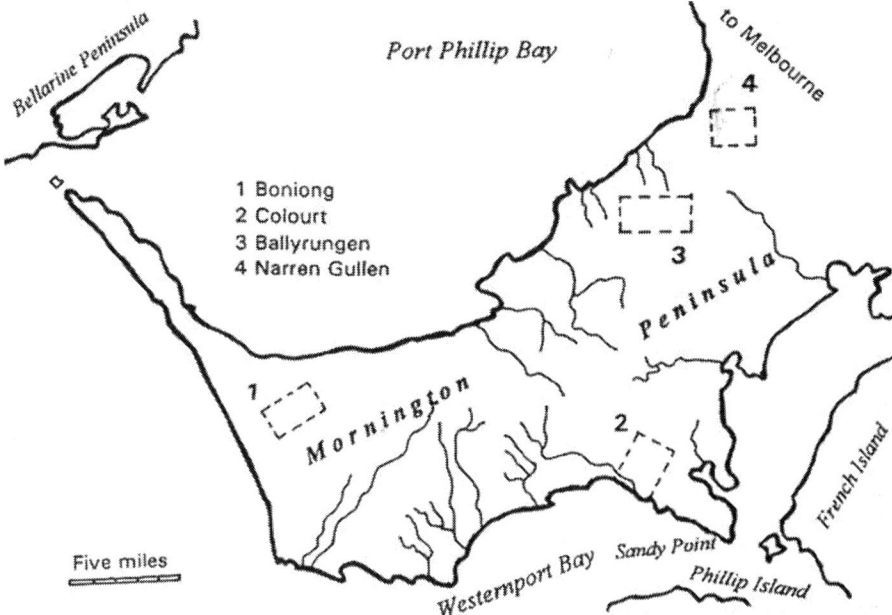

1 Boniong
2 Colourt
3 Ballyrungen
4 Narren Gullen

The Boon Wurrung aboriginal Australians lived by hunting and fishing

in food sources, not only fish and shellfish, but also a variety of animals and plant foods. The foreshores and creeks in the area were an ideal place to fish and hunt for seafood (periwinkles, mussels, etc) and for salt-water plants. The creeks also provided drinking water for the people as well as encouraging animals to the area, widening the Boon Wurrung's diet to include game such as kangaroos and possums.

From the end of the eighteenth century this wandering way of life was threatened by the arrival of Europeans. Boon Wurrung people came into contact with seal hunters and they encountered ships and sailors from the early voyages of exploration. Violence soon followed.

The first recorded contact between aboriginal Australians and Europeans in Victoria took place on the beach near Dromana in February 1802. It commenced in a friendly-enough spirit but, as so often, misunderstandings soon crept in. Spears were thrown, shots were fired, and two black men were injured, probably fatally.

European settlers brought in their own animals. Cattle and sheep overgrazed the land and destroyed much of the plant life that natives relied on for food. Kangaroos, wallabies, emus and other animals were forced back from the coast as the European animals took over. And Boon Wurrung people began to die from diseases imported by the settlers.

Now, thirty-seven years later, the Boon Wurrung had been reduced to only eighty or ninety people from a probable pre-contact population of greater than five hundred. Maurice Meyrick took the trouble to learn the local language so that he might get to know his indigenous neighbours. As a result he developed a rather different view of them from that of his ex-pat colleagues, who viewed them as little more than savages to be exterminated. This would in time lead to a degree of social discomfort for Maurice. Once, when he was out with a hunting party, he refused to fire on Boon Wurrung men—to the intense indignation of his companions.

Having taken up his run, Meyrick was full of praise for his new home and the opportunities it offered. But he was lonely. Accustomed in England to the companionship of his brothers and cousins, he wrote home to ask whether his younger brother Alfred might join him? Together they

Meyrick took the trouble to learn the Boon Wurrung language

could make their fortune and return home in five years' time. His parents discussed the proposition and it was agreed that Alfred, too, should sail for Australia. Furthermore, their even-younger cousin, Henry, would accompany him.

The two youths, nineteen and seventeen, set sail aboard *China* and arrived in Port Phillip at the end of April 1840. In Melbourne they were met by Maurice who introduced the newcomers to colonial life. The three young men managed their affairs separately, giving each other help and support when required. "We all hang together pretty well," reported cousin Henry in one of his many letters home.

The new arrivals had intended to buy sheep but during their first weeks in Melbourne they were persuaded by a friend (presumably a man with cattle to sell) to put their money into cattle instead. Sheep were too risky. Catarrh and scab were prevalent and wild dogs a continual threat. Instead the "friend" sold them eighty head of cattle each, equal numbers of cows, heifers, bullocks and yearlings, to be delivered in Melbourne from Sydney at seven pounds ten shillings per head. This was over half their total capital, a huge investment. Henry bought a horse for himself for which he paid sixty guineas—in England it would have cost him twenty-five pounds. He later admitted that they had been cheated.

Soon after arrival Alfred and Henry took up the grazing licence for Colourt, situated some sixteen miles from Maurice's run at Boniyong. At first they were enthusiastic about their land. "We found an excellent run but we shall have to clear away a marsh to get water; there is a splendid river running through the middle of it, but unfortunately it is salt. It is, however, full of fish and crammed with ducks…" Henry reported. However they soon found themselves defeated by the difficulty of draining the swamps and the hopeless search for a reliable source of fresh water.

Maurice was increasingly dissatisfied with his run at Boniyong too. The soil was sandy, the sheep pastures dry-looking and white. Prices for wool were falling. There had been a problem involving a disputed boundary and waterhole with Edward Barker, part-owner of the neighbouring run. The disagreement climaxed in a duel in 1842.

The south of the Mornington Peninsula was held at the time as large runs with the Barker brothers at Cape Schanck, Maurice Meyrick at Boniyong, and Maurice's friend Edward Hobson at Tootgarook. In 1842 John Barker had returned to England leaving his brother Dr Edward Barker, a surgeon who gave up medicine for the land, running their station at Barrabang. It was while John Barker was in England that a disagreement between Dr Barker and Maurice Meyrick led to a duel.

Accounts of the cause of the dispute vary, but in later years Barker's second insisted that the quarrel was about "the digging of a water hole at Boniyong". As in the Wild West of the United States, access to fresh water was a source of frequent dispute, often leading to violence. A furi-

Maurice Meyrick ran both sheep and cattle stations, but had little success with either

The De Salis waterhole

ous argument flared up between Meyrick and Barker. They agreed to let another neighbour, Captain Reid, settle it and, being a soldier, Reid suggested they fight it out with his duelling pistols.

On the fateful day the parties assembled at the De Salis waterhole, near the turn off to the present Cape Schanck lighthouse. Both men secretly wished that the whole affair could be called off, but their "seconds" eventually managed to get them lined up.

Duelling was outlawed soon afterwards

Meyrick fired first, his ball whistling past Barker's ear. This gave Barker such a fright that he fired wildly into the air and, the story goes, downed an unsuspecting seagull. All agreed that honour had been satisfied, and they went off to celebrate at Meyrick's house.

Then Maurice's friend Edward Hobson was forced off his run. Hitherto Crown land had been available by licence/lease for grazing purposes but several special surveys had been introduced in 1841 to allow the purchase of eight square miles (two thousand and seventy hectares) at a price well below the land value. Edward Hobson, who had the run Packomedurrawurra on the Mornington Peninsula was displaced when Robert Jamieson purchased a special survey which enveloped Hobson's run. Maurice's cousin Henry wrote home: "Hobson is sold out by one of these villainous special surveys, and I am afraid Maurice will be the next to suffer." Maurice became anxious about his tenure at Boniyong.

Other squatters with established stations were alarmed too. They were already struggling not only with the environment, but with the massive financial slump that had followed the earlier boom. Sheep that had been worth three pounds in 1839 were now valued in shillings.

Gipps Land beckoned. It was now seen as a land of promise and Maurice was convinced he would do better there than at Western Port.

The Barker station at Cape Schanck: Maurice's station would have looked very similar

A number of settlers had already moved there when, in 1844, Maurice sold up Boniyong and prepared to take his sheep, a flock of some two thousand animals, to a station on the Thompson River. Cousin Henry undertook to help him move the sheep overland while brother Alfred stayed to attend to matters on the peninsula.

Guided by Maurice's enthusiastic advice, Alfred and Henry planned to acquire two adjoining runs along the fertile flats of the McAlister River valley in mountain country. The river had to be forded no less than eleven times to reach the run which was twenty-five miles from the nearest neighbour. It was a picturesque spot, but very isolated and completely cut off during the winter months.

Gipps Land did not treat them kindly. As the months passed Maurice changed his plans once more and went to the Mitchell River, leaving Alfred and Henry feeling somewhat let down. Next, Maurice was in Sydney from where news came of his intended engagement. But nothing came of it. The story goes that the young lady, possibly a Meyrick cousin, had been trifling with his affections in order to ensnare another suitor.

Alfred had joined Henry, but suffered continued ill-health in the mountains. This prevented him from giving much assistance with the heavier work. Alfred's health so troubled Henry that he wanted to send his cousin either to Sydney or to England. Meanwhile, Henry was trying to manage the work alone—it was hard to find men to work in such an isolated spot. At the end of two years Henry was still sleeping under a tarpaulin as he strove to manage three flocks with very little help. To add to his difficulties rheumatism had crippled his left arm.

Disillusioned, Alfred and Henry sold everything but their horses, undecided about a future in Gipps Land. In May 1847, while they waited for a spell of particularly wet weather to ease, they stayed with friends the Desailly family on the Thompson River. Mrs Desailly got into difficulty while giving birth so, in torrential rain, Henry set out to fetch a

Meyrick's vicarage at Northleigh

doctor. The Desaillys' man went with Henry to the river and urged him not to cross over by the house but to go up stream.

Henry didn't listen, and he and his horse were swept downstream from the landing place. Separated from his horse, Henry appeared to go back in to the middle of the river. He may have lost his sense of direction, or he may have gone back into the flow to look for a landing place. In any event, he disappeared for ever. The horse made it across, but gave up waiting for him. It swam back and returned home with no Henry and no doctor. Consequently, Mrs Desailly died too. The two brothers, Maurice and Alfred, quit Gipps Land soon after.

After eleven years away, Maurice returned to England. His parents seem to have picked up his bills for the next few months so one assumes he did not make his fortune in the colonies as he had hoped.

At King's College London, Meyrick was ordained. He taught Latin at Queen's College in Harley Street, a school for young ladies working towards university entrance. And then at last he did what his family had expected him to do. In 1853 Maurice Meyrick was made a deacon and listed as Theological Associate of King's College London. A year after becoming a deacon he became a priest, and just a few days later, a curate in Shaftesbury. He was always involved in educational matters, and his career seems to have been bound up with Angela Burdett Coutts and her various philanthropic ventures. She lived with her father Francis at the manor in Meyrick's home village of Ramsbury in Wiltshire.

In 1864, at the age of 45, Maurice married London solicitor's daughter Eleanor Randall, 20. The couple had no children.

Maurice became vicar of Northleigh in 1883 and of Northmoor in 1885. Before anyone had the sense to challenge him to a duel, Meyrick oversaw the removal from the church in Northmoor of the old box pews, the replacement of the stone-flagged floor with wood blocks, and the scraping off of irreplaceable wall-paintings. Maurice Meyrick died in Northmoor in February 1890.

The interior of the church of St Denys, Northmoor, before Meyrick's modernisation

13

The good soldier

ON PATROL IN WALTON STREET, Oxford, one August evening in 1887 was Police Inspector Joseph Windows. At the sound of a fast-galloping horse, he turned just in time to see a man being pitched out of a trap and into the road. The man was evidently drunk.

He was Irishman Thomas Edwin Powell, fifty-eight-year-old former soldier, landlord of the Perch at Binsey, a man of (almost) unblemished character. Naturally Powell's line of work meant that he had broken up many fights, and dressed the resulting wounds. But, contrary to received stereotypes of Irish army veterans, Powell was an upstanding citizen determined to do his best to help others. So what had happened to cause him to go so dramatically off the rails?

Thomas Powell was born in Killaloe in County Clare in 1829. Killaloe stands on the River Shannon, on the southern end of Lough Derg. It boasted a

Thomas Powell

Killaloe in County Clare

square, a main street and several smaller streets, and about three hundred houses. The two weekly markets indicated a certain prosperity among the farming classes, and there was a flourishing woollen and cloth industry. Whiskey distilleries provided employment, and the Shannon Steam Navigation Company had their headquarters here and established regular communication by steam packets for goods and passengers up the Shannon. But bad times were on the way.

A famine in 1830 was the beginning of a fifteen-year period of crop failures that culminated in the crisis of 1846. The threat of starvation became an annual event, and was often accompanied by outbreaks of cholera. Terrorist groups like the Rockites and the Terry Alts blamed the British government and targeted anyone supporting authority. For many young men, the best escape was to join the army.

Thomas enlisted in 21st (Royal North British) Fusiliers Regiment of Foot as Private 2588 when the regiment returned home from India at the height of the potato famine in 1848. In the following year he was based at Leith Fort in Edinburgh where he married an Irish labourer's daughter, seventeen-year-old Elizabeth White. In her photograph

Elizabeth looks sweet and compliant, but she will have known that the life of an army wife would be tough, and in time she gave birth in four different countries.

Elizabeth's first baby, Thomas was born in 1851, but he seems to have died as an infant. After that, the couple probably decided to wait to have more children; there was trouble in the east, and the army would be needed. The British government was concerned to contain Russian expansionism, and the Ottoman Empire needed help to retain control of the Crimea.

In June 1853, the 21st Foot went to Ireland, perhaps on a recruiting drive, sailing from Hull to Dublin. In August 1854, they embarked at Cork for the Black Sea. The Crimean War was the last in which wives were permitted to follow their husbands. Places for four army wives out of every hundred were allotted by ballot, but either way the arrangements for women were virtually non-existent. If they remained at home they were thrown out of the barracks, if they went to the Crimea they

Leith Fort in Edinburgh

Thomas's wife Elizabeth

were crammed with the rest of the soldiery into make-shift huts. The lack of Powell babies during this period suggests that Elizabeth stayed behind.

Thomas fought at the Battles of Alma, and was wounded at Inkerman, and at the assault on the Redan at Sevastopol. He also fought at Balaklava. In June 1856, the 21st embarked from Balaklava for Malta where evidently Thomas and his wife were reunited because Elizabeth gave birth at the Valetta garrison to James Henry in 1857 and Thomas John in 1859. Thomas senior signed on for another eleven years.

When the regiment removed to the West Indies, Elizabeth gave birth to Elizabeth Mary in Barbados. They came home in 1864, and William Denis was born at Portsmouth in 1865. In September 1866 the 21st Foot was deployed to Ireland, where Francis Frederick and then Joseph Patrick appeared.

In February 1869, the 21st Foot set off for Bombay, but, at the age of around forty-two and with a wife and six young children, Thomas remained in Ireland. He transferred to Royal Tyrone Fusiliers, and then came to England where for ten years he was a sergeant in the Oxford Militia in its new, Gothic-style fort on Bullingdon Green. The Powell family, including all six children, lived in a small, terraced villa in

Cowley Barracks, originally "Bullingdon" Barracks

Magdalen Road in the new suburb of Cowley. With decent schools and no risk of famine, the Powells no doubt felt that they were giving their children a better start in life than they had themselves enjoyed.

Thomas launched into civilian life determined upon respectability. He joined the Cowley Conservative Association and, when the license for the Old Dog and Tray public house in Red Lion Street by Gloucester Green became available at the start of November 1876, Thomas acquired it.

This was good timing because Wombwell's Menagerie was due to set up camp in Gloucester Green a few weeks later, so trade would be brisk during the show. From 6–9 December, performances by trained bears, wolves, hyenas, leopards, panthers and elephants were promised, but not, as it turned out, by one unfortunate camel.

In mid December, Thomas's servant Elizabeth Bull opened the door of the stables at the Old Dog and Tray and found a dead camel decomposing gently. Thomas had evidently obliged the proprietor of the travelling circus by providing somewhere to stow the expired artiste. On the 21st Elizabeth also died following several days of suffering from con-

Travelling menageries of exotic beasts were a popular attraction

stant diarrhoea. Such an offensive smell, it was decided at her inquest, could easily have accelerated death in a lady already experiencing ulceration of the lower intestine and an abscess in the pelvis. Thomas's good deed had gone horribly wrong.

Thomas came to the rescue again in 1879 when a fight outside his pub in Gloucester Green resulted in a nasty wound to the face of one of the participants. Powell took the man inside and little Elizabeth washed the wound. And with more space in the pub than there had been in Magdalen Road, Thomas had taken in a colleague from the 21st Regiment, Irishman John Burke. Like Thomas, Burke had fought at Sevastopol, and like some servicemen even today, now apparently he had nowhere to call home.

Another old soldier who had reason to be grateful to Thomas Powell was Joseph Kavanagh, an Irishman who also fought at Inkerman in the Crimea. He sustained a wound to the leg that caused him to be discharged, and thereafter he found it impossible to settle. Today he might be considered in need of some kind of psychological help, but in those days there was nothing. By 1874, Kavanagh had already been convicted nine times in Oxford city court for begging, drinking, and getting into fights. In February 1879 he was even charged for "wandering about", though this may suggest that a kind police officer thought some hot soup and a night in a warm cell was in order. When Kavanagh died in 1885, *Jackson's Oxford Journal* revealed that he "was greatly indebted to the kindness of Sergt T Powell, landlord of the Old Dog and Tray, Gloucester-street, who always gave him shelter, and proved to the last a true friend to an old comrade".

A move out to the picturesque Perch Inn in the idyllic village of Binsey must have seemed to Thomas and Elizabeth the summit of their dreams. Their eldest son James had married and moved away with his family to Staines. Two other sons, Joseph and Francis came with their parents to Binsey—even John Burke was still in the household, along with three lodgers. But things were beginning to go wrong in the family.

Daughter Elizabeth had been married to army pensioner Francis Robinson in 1881, and by 1882 he was already in gaol. Only twenty-

The Perch at Binsey

Mary Robinson and her son Francis

one at the time of his marriage, Francis's army pension cannot have amounted to much, and he worked as a telegraph operator for the post office. Perhaps anxious about his duty to support a wife, young Francis stole fifty-seven pounds from the post office, plus a postal order for eleven shillings. He was sentenced to five years' penal servitude, the enlightened substitute for transportation.

Elizabeth began to use her other name, Mary, and to call herself a widow. She moved in with her parents at the Perch, along with her son Francis. The lad was born in Binsey in 1886—four years *after* her husband's detention. Evidently Francis Robinson was not the boy's father. But this was not all.

In 1877, second son John had enlisted at eighteen in the Royal Engineers where he was trained as a telegrapher. Upon his discharge, he went to work on the Manchester Ship Canal. Navvies were well-paid, but they worked long hours in very difficult conditions. In the beating sun or the pouring rain, they broke their backs hand-shovelling millions of tonnes of rock and soil to create the waterway. Over one hundred and thirty men were killed and hundreds more were disfigured or disabled due to the back-breaking nature of the work. John could tolerate only so much before he began to look round for get-rich-quick schemes.

John's criminal record is difficult to untangle because he used the alias of Richard Parker, and maybe others too. Indeed, he may even have swapped identities with a genuine Richard Parker when it suited them. On 7 May 1886 he was sentenced at Chester Assizes to two months' hard labour for burglary. Afterwards he came home to the Perch, but mysteriously "fell through a window" on Christmas Eve. One can't help picturing Thomas Powell pitching his recalcitrant son out of the pub via the window.

In April 1887 Thomas was summonsed for hard swearing and fighting with one of his own customers. The man who had so often broken up fights was now at the centre of one. But he probably knew that his son John was in trouble again. On 6 May, John was sentenced at Stafford to six months' hard labour yet again for another burglary. And it was during this second prison term that his father Thomas drove so furiously down Walton Street and landed on his head in the road. A repentant Thomas Powell not only paid his court fine and costs, but he donated ten shillings to the Radcliffe Infirmary who had, presumably, patched him up.

Following his latest release, John came home again, and in the summer of 1888 he was bound over for using threats towards his father. Predictably he did not last long at home.

Many Irish former-soldiers found work digging the Manchester Ship Canal

Thomas was mortified that he had fallen foul of the law in Walton Street in Oxford

In September 1889, John left his job on the canal and gave burglary another whirl. A couple of watches, and some silver bits and pieces cost him a further month in gaol, after which he made his way back to Binsey. This time, his father did not turn his disappointing son away, but John was obliged to make his home in one of the outhouses belonging to the pub. One can only imagine the frustration for Thomas, who had escaped famine-torn Ireland for a gruelling thirty years in the army in order to provide his children with a comparatively comfortable life in Oxford.

Thomas Powell, the Crimea veteran, recipient of numerous good conduct badges, who more-or-less defied the stereotype of the feckless, drunken trouble-making Irishman, died aged sixty-seven in 1896 still providing a home for his old comrade John Burke. Only the signal failure of his son John to capitalise on the advantages life offered him in prosperous Oxfordshire shook his determination upon respectability.

His doughty wife Elizabeth took over the license at the Perch until her death in 1903.

14

The Bampton inventor

WITH TYPICAL EDWARDIAN gusto at the beginning of the twentieth century, a young entrepreneur in a bicycle shop embraced the modern age, and produced the first Oxfordshire motorcar. No, not William Morris—the rather less well-known Onesiphorus Oliver Collett of Bampton.

Onesiphorus was born in July 1869; his father William Collett farmed fifty-six acres at Weald at the western end of Bampton, employing three men and a boy. By the time Onesiphorus was eleven, William was sixty-four; he had given up most of his land, and described himself as a miller with about four acres.

Horse power still ruled when Onesiphorus grew up in Bampton

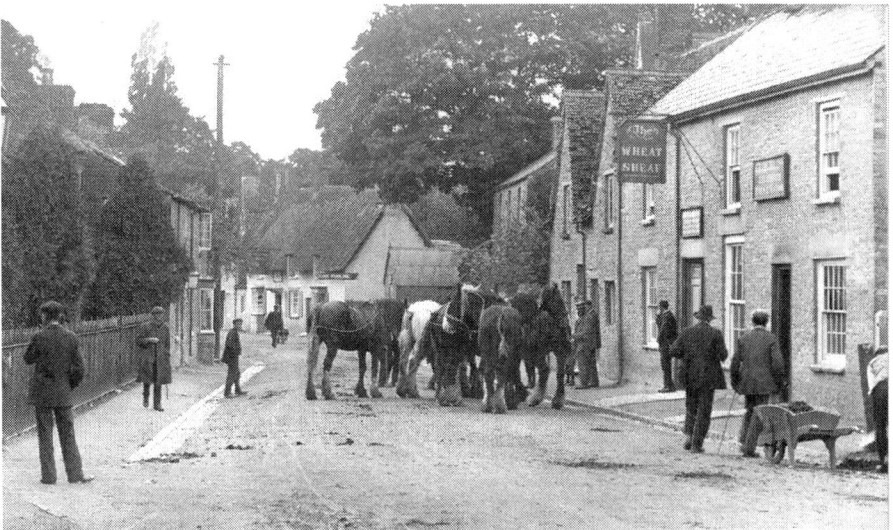

Collett's watch-repair and jewellery business in Cheapside, Bampton

William died aged seventy-three at the beginning of 1888. In the same year nineteen-year-old Onesiphorus leased a shop in Cheapside, now known as Exeter House, and opened a watch-repair and jewellery business. His mother and two of his sisters had a draper's shop next door. This may have been the point at which Onesiphorus found it more convenient to abandon his cumbersome first name (a biblical one meaning 'benefit-bringer') and use the simpler 'Oliver'.

The advent of machine-made parts and the necessity, in an age now governed by railway timetables, to keep accurate time meant that a watch was both affordable and essential to the working man. Age-old but imprecise markers like sunrise and sunset would no longer do, and the chimes of the church clock may not be so easily heard in noisy workshops as they were for those who still laboured out in the fields. Onesiphorus prospered.

But it was really transport that was the obsession of the age. The advent of the "safety bicycle" in the 1880s made this mode of locomotion far less hazardous than previously, and the relatively low cost of the bicycle brought independent travel for work or pleasure within the means of ordinary people—even ladies. Within months of opening his shop, Onesiphorus began building bicycles and tricycles, and even deployed his engineering skills to design a dual-powered bicycle.

A stiff left leg resulting from a childhood fall out of a tree meant that he had difficulty riding a conventional cycle; the new design involved a drive-cog above the handlebars with a chain running down to another

Onesiphorus shows off his innovative bicycle design, adapted for his stiff left leg

Motorising the bicycle was the next step

cog on the front wheel. This drive-cog was activated by short cranks con-
nected to the handlebar. By pumping these cranks up and down power
was delivered to the front wheel.

Motorcycles were the next obvious progression for Collett, and his
design even had a convenient sidecar—the first to be seen in the district. A four-wheeled, two-seater quadricycle with a steering wheel, as
demonstrated in the photo by his wife and sister, was a clear indicator
of things to come, though fortunately the notion of positioning the passenger immediately in front of the driver's eye-line was not pursued.

In 1899, at the age of 30, Onesiphorus acquired a wife. Through business connections with other young men of similar interests, he met Mary
Warner. Mary lived with her widowed mother in Witney; her brother
Robert ran a cycle shop and another brother, John, was a watchmaker.
A third brother, Alfred, was also engineering-mad, and would eventually set up in Market Street, Charlbury as a "motor and cycle maker",
according to the 1911 census. Onesiphorus and Mary would have two
children: Ethel in 1900, and Christopher in 1911.

Onesiphorus needed bigger premises to match his expanding plans, and in 1900 he acquired the lease on the blacksmith's premises next door at Cromwell House. And this was when his most ambitious plan came to fruition—ten years ahead of William Morris's 'Bullnose' Morris. For Collett designed and built a motorcar—the 'Bampton Voiturette'. The engine was placed in front of the radiator in the typical Franco-Belgian fashion favoured by Renault. This enabled the radiator to keep the passengers warm. Light wheels, handlebar steering and twin carriage-lights made the Voiturette more advanced than other motors being designed at the time.

But motorcars were still seen as rich men's playthings. And unfortunately there were no rich men around in Bampton with the vision to invest in Collett's design so early, whereas within a few years both William Morris in Oxford and Henry Royce in Manchester found backers. This negative attitude, coupled with a period of recession in 1907,

The "Bampton Voiturette", as demonstrated by the Collett family and their assistant

William Morris's factory at Cowley in 1913...

resulted in Onesiphorus abandoning his plans to build motor vehicles by 1908 and, after a couple of years, he dismantled his beloved Voiturette. Meanwhile in 1912, William Morris began assembling cars; within fifteen years his factory at Cowley was producing 1,500 cars a week.

From his car, Collett kept the engine which now provided electric lighting for his house (a breath-taking innovation in Bampton!) and recharged his customers' wireless batteries. From now on, he focused on the business of maintaining and servicing vehicles in his workshop and secured franchises for Palmer Cord Tyres, Pratt's Perfection Spirit, and Gargoyle Mobiloil.

However, once an inventor, always an inventor. Because of his age and slight disability, Onesiphorus received no call-up papers during the First World War. Upon hearing that soldiers in the trenches were making tea over a candle stuck in a cocoa tin, Onesiphorus realised that not only was this method of heating liquids inefficient, it rendered the troops vulnerable to snipers on account of the glow from the lighted candle. He decided to make a contribution to their safety and comfort. He hit on the solution of channelling the heat upwards through the tin by means of a funnel which also obscured the bright light of the candle.

His daughter Ethel recalls: 'We got everyone to give us their spare tins and my father and mother and I spent ages soldering the new bits in and we stuck some wire on top as a holder. We worked in his workshop until late in the evening and sometimes packed a hundred and twenty of them off to the Tommies as our family contribution to the parcel, along with the fruit cakes and the tobacco from everyone else. It was a good idea too, because several of the men when they came back said they had been glad to have the Collett cocoa tins.'

With his sister Susannah, Onesiphorus even launched a medicinal lotion. "Collett's Salve"—"the best known for gatherings, broken chilblains, burns scalds, etc." was made to a family recipe and could, apparently, be used "without fear on the most delicate skin of children".

In 1922 with the launch of the radio and the British Broadcasting

... and Collett's Voiturette, abandoned for spares

In the 1950s, Onesiphorus's son Christopher sold petrol to happy Morris customers

Corporation, Oliver immediately spotted another business opportunity and added "wireless set repairs" to his many skills. It was also around this time that he installed a petrol pump at his Cheapside garage, no doubt a considerable boon to all those happy owners of Morris motorcars.

After a lifetime of innovation, Collett died on 13 March 1934, described simply as a "watchmaker". His son Christopher continued in the business until after the Second World War, when the business was bought out. By the 1950s, regular daily buses carried workers from Bampton Market Place to the Morris factory at Cowley.

Both William Morris and Onesiphorus Collett built bicycle and motorcycle businesses. Both men had creative, inventive and visionary minds, but only one had the right product, at the right time, in the right place, and at the right price. And it wasn't Onesiphorus Collett.

15

The Attagirl

ANYONE CLASSIFYING Freydis Leaf Sharland of Benson as just another little old lady in a wheelchair needed a rethink. The village was proud to be the final home of this extraordinary and brave woman.

As conflict loomed in Europe in 1939, nineteen year-old Freydis Leaf, as she then was, responded in an unusual way. As a pilot in the Air Transport Auxiliary (ATA) she went in the space of a few weeks from novice pilot to ferrying hundreds of aircraft from factories to RAF bases across Britain, and later to France and Italy.

The thing was, although Freydis came from a modest background (her father was a Cambridge University archaeologist), she happened to know how to fly already. "My father and brother,

Freydis Sharland, née Leaf

Derek, learned to fly at Marshall's Flying School on the outskirts of Cambridge," she told *Candia* magazine. "I'd always had a sense of adventure and begged my father to let me learn too, but at first he refused. However, I pestered him so much he finally agreed. I had twelve hours of training before I flew solo for the first time."

Advertisement for Marshalls' Flying School

The first flight with the instructor

At
MARSHALLS'
FLYING SCHOOL
CAMBRIDGE

Each aircraft of the fleet is of a well-proven British type, designed and developed for producing good pilots qualified to fly any modern aeroplane. Every machine is maintained in a perfect state of airworthiness by a skilled ground staff adhering implicitly to the most stringent safety regulations.

"Once the war started all civil flying stopped so I couldn't do any more," Freydis recalled in 2009. "Father joined the Barrage Balloon Battalion and my brother was already in the 'Wavy Navy', the Royal Naval Volunteer Reserve. At the outbreak of war I was living in Twickenham. My mother was in a Red Cross group and I worked in the Voluntary Aid Detachment in a military hospital in Colchester for about a year. I was dying to get into the Air Transport Auxiliary (ATA) but every time I wrote to them they said no. My four hours and forty [minutes] solo was not enough. It wasn't until the beginning of 1942 that they ran out of people with more flying than me and they gave me a flight test at White Waltham aerodrome.

"The instructor told me to take over the plane, start up the engine and take off which I did. Then we did some circuits and we flew, climbed and descended and various other manoeuvres he asked me to perform. All the time I kept an eye on where the aerodrome was because, I thought, 'I bet he'll ask me to find my way home.' Which eventually he did. I knew exactly where it was so I turned to the aerodrome and flew home. I did a circuit there and landed, went into the clubhouse and waited. Then I heard I had passed my flying test and they would try to get me into the ATA."

The Air Transport Auxiliary was a civilian organisation set up in September 1939 to ferry new, repaired and damaged military aircraft between factories, assembly plants, and maintenance depots to active service squadrons and airfields, as well as transporting service personnel on urgent duty and performing some air ambulance work.

The idea of utilising civilian ferry pilots was first suggested by Gerard d'Erlanger, a banker and director of British Airways, and Sir Francis Shelmerdine, director-general of civil aviation. And by August 1941 the ATA had taken over all ferrying responsibility, freeing up much-needed pilots for combat roles.

In November 1942 Freydis joined the service, aged twenty-two. She became one of only two female civilian trainees for the ATA at Barton-in-the-Clay, north of the Chilterns. She trained on bi-planes such as the Hawker Hart and monoplanes like the Fairchild Angus, and moved on to Tiger Moths and Fairey Swordfish before being posted to RAF Cosford near Birmingham, where she was a member of Number 12 Ferry Pilots' Pool, one of only two such pools staffed entirely by women.

"My first job was to ferry a Tiger Moth up to a base in Shropshire," she recalls, "but unfortunately I went the wrong way. I got there in the end!"

Freydis accumulated over six hundred and seven hours in the wartime sky carrying out various tasks the length and breadth of Britain. She started out on Magister trainers and graduated to twin-engined bombers such as the Vickers Wellington, the Lockheed Hudson and the ultra-fast, and tricky, De Havilland Mosquito. Then there were the frontline fighters, Hurricanes and Spitfires.

"We got quite keen on flying new types and there was a lot of competition, with everyone trying to fly as many aeroplanes as they could," Freydis revealed in an interview in 2009. "It was always interesting in the morning when you got your chits. These told you what they wanted

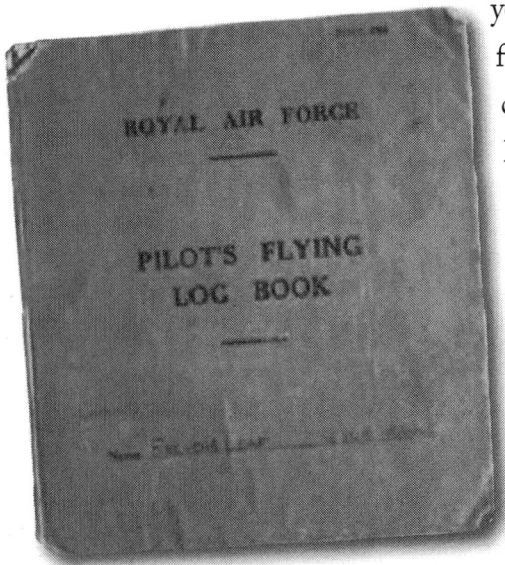

you to fly and where to." She flew thirty-eight different aircraft types but confirms that her favourite aeroplane was the Spitfire.

"Gosh, it felt like someone had kicked me in the rear end, and the next thing I knew I was at a thousand feet! It was unlike anything we'd ever flown. It was so light, so manoeuvrable and you fitted

Checking the route in the cockpit of a Fairchild Argus

into it so well, it was such a nice little cockpit. It was quite fast, so you had to take extra care in bad weather," she explained.

"The Mosquito was quite hard to fly. Once the wheels and flaps were down it had quite a high stalling speed and you had to be very careful to keep well above that speed otherwise 'Ping!'—one day you'd hit the ground and that would be the end of you."

The rule was that ATA pilots avoided flying in bad weather. They were not supposed to set off unless the cloud base was at least eight hundred feet, and horizontal visibility two thousand yards. (These limitations were probably as much about saving money and training time as preventing the enemy from detecting their movements.) The reality was rather different, and pioneer flier Amy Johnson became the first woman in the ATA to die when she baled out in cloud over the Thames estuary in January 1941.

Fifteen women died flying with the ATA. Navigation meant skilled,

Just like the men, the women pilots endured long waits

solo map reading, and tracking destinations by railway lines, lakes, and gasometers. There were other dangers, too. Flying a Tiger Moth, Freydis was turned over by the slipstream of a giant, four-engined Liberator bomber.

"I was delivering it to a place in Wales and I could see all these Liberators lined up and one of them had started his engine. I should have stopped and waited for someone to hold my aeroplane but I didn't. I thought I'd try and rush along behind him and get through, but of course I didn't. The Tiger Moth was a very flimsy little aircraft and the slipstream just turned me over. That was rather bad. It wasn't too badly damaged—just the wings and the propeller, but I had to deliver it in a rather miserable state and I was responsible for it, which was a black mark on my record."

"Our greatest enemy was the weather," she confirmed. "Lots of my friends lost their lives by crashing into hills in poor conditions. The next morning their name would be scrubbed off the board in the office, and the place would be horribly quiet. The truth is, I tried for years not to remember what we went through. When I think back I still get sleepless nights, and the heart starts racing." Yet ATA fliers all took chances with

Britain's unpredictable weather; the service would have ground to a halt if they had not.

Initially, as the pilots were civilian and/or women, the aircraft were ferried with unloaded guns or other armaments. Because they were required to stay within sight of the ground, they were not taught the art of flying with instruments. They flew "blind" with just maps, a compass and a watch, though some would eventually make it their business to teach themselves instrument flying by scrounging sessions in an early flight simulator called a Link Trainer. It wasn't until after D-Day in June 1944 that pilots were taught how to use radios. However, after encounters with German aircraft in which the ferried aircraft were unable to fight back, RAF aircraft were then ferried with guns fully loaded.

"Fortunately," Freydis observed: "I never had to shoot down a German. There wasn't one available at the time."

The ATA was one of the few diverse organisations during the war.

Women pilots worked twelve days on, two days off (Freydis sits at the back)

Apart from accepting women as well as men, there were disabled pilots, older pilots and people of many nationalities, including from neutral countries. Twenty-eight different nationalities flew with the ATA. Freydis acknowledged that, thanks to the efforts of her fellow flyers, and those of Sir Stafford Cripps, minister of aircraft production, the ATA pioneered equal pay. She had never before, she observed, had so much money in her life. At the same time, American women flying with the Women Airforce Service Pilots received as little as sixty-five per cent of their equivalent male colleagues.

The challenges the Attagirls faced were extraordinary because ATA pilots were not specifically trained to fly the many different types of war planes they were expected to transport. Sometimes pilots would fly six different types of plane in just one day, ferrying Spitfires, Hurricanes, Barracudas, Harvards, Wellingtons, Tempests and Lancaster bombers in the ever-changing British weather without radios or navigation aids. Instead, after some very limited training in the air, they were handed a small book known as the "ferry pilot's notes", which contained all the technical data they needed to know to fly each different plane. Women like Freydis, who flew thirty-eight different types of aircraft, were forced constantly to refer to these notes to work out how to use the muddle of flying instruments in front of them.

Freydis herself rarely complained about sexist behaviour, but a male member of the RAF once made a complaint about another Attagirl after observing her reading while she was piloting the plane he was on. He reportedly said of the journey: "It was dreadful weather and I can't believe that, not only was a woman flying me, but she was reading a book." The pilot's response was that no, those were her ATA notes. She hadn't flown that type of plane before. Apparently, upon hearing this, the disgruntled passenger nearly lost his lunch.

Another Oxfordshire Attagirl, Mary Ellis of Leafield, told the story of the day she landed a Wellington bomber. "Where's the pilot?" demanded

Freydis B. Shaoland
Ferry pilot A.T.A.

Freydis was called upon to sign endless photographs of Spitfires

an amazed RAF ground crew. "I *am* the pilot," replied ATA First Officer Ellis. Unconvinced, the men searched the aircraft, just to be sure.

ATA ferry pilots faced a death rate of one in ten but, in spite of the risks, their motto was "eager for the air". Freydis's fellow Attagirl Jayne Edwards once explained: "To take off, especially on a bright day, and then be at two thousand feet, the sun shining, no clouds, just you—it was fabulous. The war didn't exist. It was just—'*wow*'".

Freydis lost her elder brother and seven cousins between 1939 and 1945. At a ceremony on 30 November 1945, the ATA's flag was lowered for the last time. Its role was vital to the success of the RAF in World War II and to the outcome of the war. Said Lord Beaverbrook on the occasion: "Just as the Battle of Britain is the accomplishment and achievement of the RAF, likewise it can be declared that the ATA sustained and supported them in battle. They were soldiers fighting in the struggle just as completely as if they had been engaged on the battlefront." But Freydis's flying career had hardly begun. She served as a pilot in the WRAF VR (Reserves) in the late 1940s and early 1950s, and earned, but did not collect, her RAF "wings", saying she looked lanky in the uniform.

In 1953 Freydis Leaf climbed into a 430mph Hawker Tempest V, and set off from an airfield in southern England on a four thousand-mile intercontinental flight. Her aeroplane was one of the biggest and fastest of the last generation of piston-engined RAF fighters, and her destination was Pakistan. Leaf's stopovers, an itinerary for the last days of empire, took in Nicosia, Baghdad—where she was entranced by the almond trees—and Bahrain, and then she undertook the final, and longest, leg to Karachi. After enduring two weeks of privation, and having delivered the Tempest to the Pakistan Air Force, she asked if she might pop in to the officer's mess for a cup of tea. Her request was denied. She was, after all, only a woman.

Freydis painted her racing number onto her aircraft herself

Racing replaced the thrill of wartime flying

She worked as a freelance commercial pilot, and around 1952, she began racing aeroplanes. "I painted 45—my racing number—on the side of the plane myself," she recalls. In 1954, Freydis entered the British Air Racing Championship. A typical handicapped air racing season, it embraces some eight venues and sixteen races; the maximum points available for a win in each race is one hundred. Defeating sixteen men in this cumulative championship in a Hawk Major, Freydis won and became the first woman to hold the title.

It was on the *Edinburgh Castle* liner to South Africa with her mother on her way to visit her younger brother Robin in the following year that she met former British army lieutenant, Tim Sharland.

"He was a lieutenant with the British Army, but had left to farm in Africa," Freydis explains. "We got on extremely well and married just a few months later on New Year's Eve 1955 near Durban."

Freydis's final home in Benson

The couple ran a farm in what was then Northern Rhodesia, now Zambia. "We had sheep, cows and lots of fruit. Luckily, Tim didn't mind me flying, so I renewed my licence and took several trips across Africa until I fell pregnant with our first child. Eventually we returned to the UK where we bought a small farm in Buckinghamshire and our second daughter was born, followed by our son."

"As soon as I could, I went back to the air and returned to working with the female cadets. I retired at sixty, but I bought a microlight and kept flying until I was seventy-two."

Upon retirement, Freydis and her husband settled in Brook Street in Benson. She lived out her last years enjoying the familiar background sounds of the nearby airfield at RAF Benson.

"The cottage where we live now lies in the shadow of an aerodrome and our days are punctuated by the noise of planes. I love the sound, it takes me back to days gone by."

Freydis Sharland died in May 2014.

16

The wartime decoy

ANY LADY OF A CERTAIN AGE who lives alone and eschews the blessings of a husband, who has no children in view and sustains herself by unknown financial means is guaranteed to be considered by her neighbours "eccentric". It has been so throughout the ages. And if that lady should be so reckless as to betray a superior intellect, the die is firmly cast. Such a one was Charlotte Ann Partridge of Upton near Blewbury.

Following the death of her father, she rattled about alone at Frogalley Farm some way along a muddy lane out of Upton, a site now sadly der-

The Crossings at Stream Road, leading to Frog Alley and Frogalley Farm

elict. Every day without fail two other spinster ladies called upon Miss Partridge. Susanna and Sophie Fry from the manor house staggered up Stream Road to Frog Alley Lane lugging a large basket of food. This was not for Miss Partridge, but for the sea of cats through which she constantly waded.

The Fry sisters were talented and cultured; they trained the church choir, played the organ, and gave music lessons. Their nephew Joseph Fry, a driver for the Royal Field Artillery in World War I, was a professional musician and composer. The Frys probably found kindred spirits in the Partridges.

Charlotte was the daughter of a professor at the Guildhall School of Music in London. James Partridge had been born the son of a Staffordshire innkeeper, but his talent had taken him to London to study at the Royal Academy of Music. Charlotte Ann was born in Blomfield Road, Chelsea in 1875, and in 1885 her father graduated from assistant professor to full professor at the Guildhall School of Music.

Charlotte had three brothers. The eldest also became a teacher of music, the younger two went into the burgeoning motor trade. Following the death of Charlotte's mother in 1921, she moved with her father from west London to Frogalley Farm.

Charlotte Partridge's childhood home

What brought the Partridges to Upton is unclear, unless it was some prior professional connection between James and Joseph Fry; both were organists. The only other tenuous connection with the area unearthed so far is that James had in-laws, the Robertsons, in Shutford West near Banbury. Hardly a strong connection to a village then in Berkshire.

Charlotte's father appears in the electoral register for Upton in 1937 but he is absent from the 1939 register. So, at the outbreak of the Second World War, Miss Partridge was sixty-four and living alone at Frogalley Farm, probably in one of her own farm cottages rather than the big farmhouse. In the neighbouring cottage were retired farm worker George Bursey and his wife Emma, both in their late seventies.

Like every village and hamlet in England, Upton was on a war footing. The RAF had helpfully given some Luftwaffe big-wigs a tour of their nearby airbase at Harwell in 1938 so, hardly surprisingly, there were numerous attacks on the airfield from August 1940 onwards. A couple of very damaging raids in that first month killed two airmen and six civilians. Then, in November 1940, a Junkers-88 bomber attempted to attack the same airfield. It was intercepted over Upton by two Spit-

The RAF gave the Luftwaffe a useful tour of Harwell airfield in 1938

A Junkers-88 was forced down at Woodway Farm near Blewbury in November 1940

fires and forced down with the loss of one German airman at Woodway Farm near Blewbury. The damaged aircraft was subsequently displayed for a fortnight in St Giles Street in Oxford.

Things had gone quiet through the winter months, but in February attacks began to escalate once more. Most rural cottages still had only paraffin lamps and candles as their means of lighting, but these might still attract attention after dark. Air raid warden Alfred Newman would go about his regular evening patrol, keen to ensure that no chink of light was visible that might guide the Luftwaffe to Harwell.

There was just one resident in Upton who seemed incapable of grasping the necessity of following the black-out regulations. Charlotte Partridge refused to believe that these tiresome restrictions should apply to her because she lived such a long way from the heart of the village. Mr Newman had been obliged to speak to her about the situation on several occasions, but on the evening of 9 March 1941 he decided against trudging up to Frog Alley just to check on one light.

Charlotte Partridge was in the habit of popping out for a brisk walk up the lane and back before calling in at her outside privy on her way to bed. On darker evenings she would carry a paraffin lantern to see her way around any puddles.

At around 8.30pm, Miss Partridge was half-way back down Pink Hedge Lane when a Junkers-88 German bomber laden with five hundred incendiary devices and two five-hundred pound bombs flew in over Blewbury. Heavy air raids taking place at the same time in the Midlands and on the south coast gave the crew, whose target was again the airfield at Harwell, the cover they needed to make their way undetected across country.

Inside the noisy plane the navigator was tense; he knew his course would take him close to is target and he was waiting for a break in the cloud so that he might pick out anything that would indicate a working airfield. As he came in over Blewbury the cloud broke and down below he picked out two lights. This was it.

Except it wasn't. One light was the paraffin lamp Miss Partridge had left burning in her cottage, and the other was the lantern Charlotte carried as she scuttled back down the lane. To a navigator, the lantern looked just like a slow-moving vehicle. Confident that he had located his target, he ordered the pilot to swing north towards Didcot, then turn and strafe the airfield from north to south. The plan was probably

A Junkers-88

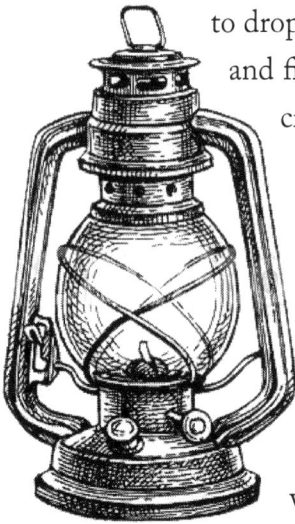

to drop the incendiaries across the accommodation area and finish by dropping the two big bombs on the aircraft hangers. Then they would run for home.

Unaware whether the plane overhead was friend or foe as it began its turn over Hagbourne, Miss Partridge decided that it was such a pleasant evening that she would continue on down the lane past her cottage for a little extra exercise. As the Junkers-88 headed back towards Upton only the slow-moving light was now visible. The navigator assumed that it identified the presence of a vehicle on the road that ran past the airfield. The aircraft drew level with the bobbing light and the crew released the incendiary bombs.

The first devices to be dropped fell on Frog Alley and one of them spiralled away towards the cottages, exploding right outside Miss Partridge's privy and setting fire to the wooden door. Had she not decided to extend her evening walk, Charlotte would have been enthroned within, with consequences too awful to contemplate.

The rest of the incendiaries fell relatively harmlessly on to Frank Napper's apple orchard between Frog Alley and Coffin Way. They were fitted with small fins that caused them to spiral as they fell so

Frank Napper

156

Upton Manor, home of the Fry family since the 1880s

that they spread out over a wide area, setting fire to many of the trees and resulting in a swathe of damage some two hundred yards wide.

At the manor one of the sisters Fry looked out of the window as the incendiaries lit up the orchard, and exclaimed: "Oh, what pretty lights!"

Her nephew Joseph, officer in charge of the local home guard, pulled her to safety just in time. When the two big bombs were released, they fell only yards from the manor house. Ten windows blew in to the rooms, and valuable china and porcelain leapt off shelves and tables, but happily Miss Fry was unharmed.

Joseph Fry: nephew of the Misses Fry, he pulled one of them to safety just in time

Frank Napper's son Guy, who had been driving his Austin 7 towards the village at the time of the attack, was one of the first people on the scene. He was soon joined by a swarm of villagers, all keen to see the extent of the damage and to grab any souvenirs before the Military Police got there to seal off the site. The whole area was illuminated by the remaining fires from the incendiaries—some forty trees burning like giant candles.

Most of the souvenir hunters were content to scamper off with fragments of the big bombs or perhaps a distorted and burnt-out incendiary case. But some of the incendiaries were slowed by the branches of the fruit trees and a soft landing on wet ground meant that they did not explode. One or two intrepid types decided that an unexploded incendiary was more interesting than a boring old fragment of metal, and several of the devices were secreted away. The farmer's son took six and immersed them in a water tank behind Owlscote Farm.

Meanwhile, Mr Newman and his team of firewatchers had gone down to deal with the fire at Frogalley Farm. Naturally greatly shocked by the explosions, Miss Partridge had galloped back to her cottage in desperate need of the privy—only to find her access barred by the burning door. It must have been a bewildering moment.

As for the Junkers-88, village legend has it that the aircraft pulled up and away towards the east. Looking back on burning fruit trees instead of a ruined airfield, the crew realised they had scored an embarrassing miss. They were tracked back across country and intercepted by a Spitfire as they crossed the east coast. It is said that the bomber was brought down, crashing into the sea with all members of the crew reported missing, presumed dead. But reports are conflicting. The only near-corresponding ditching that the present author has so far found is listed in Neil R Storey's *Norfolk in the Second World War*. On the following day, 10 March 1941, Storey

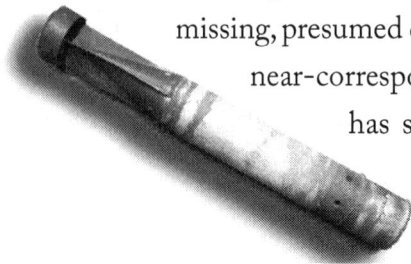

Owlscote Farm

says that Ju88A-5 (8180) of Luftwaffe bomber wing 1/KG30 ditched off-shore at Sparrow Gap near Weybourne on the Norfolk coast and the aircraft was captured.

Back in Upton, the farmer's son, an adventurous and inquisitive chap, decided to try his hand at a little bomb disposal. Over the next few days he managed to dismantle the devices he had squirrelled away, keeping the undamaged cases as treasured possessions.

At the parish meeting on 17 March, Alfred Newman thanked all the parishioners who had turned out to help on the evening of the bombing. Little did he know that certain dangerous souvenirs were still secreted around the village, or that shady bomb disposal activities were taking place behind Owlscote Farm. For his services to the village over many years, Alfred Newman was honoured by the naming of Newman's Close.

For Miss Partridge, who had single-handedly provided a decoy that probably saved the lives of many airfield personnel as well as sparing valuable aircraft and saving the country a huge repair bill, her only reward was a thorough telling-off from Alfred Newman.

Frogalley Farm barn in 1994: hardly anything remains today

Charlotte Ann Partridge remained at Frogalley Farm until she died in 1954 aged seventy-nine. After this it was demolished, and only a few tumbledown out-buildings now remain. At the manor Sophie Fry passed away first, dying aged 85 in 1946. Her sister Susanna died at the age of eighty-nine in 1957, run over by a milk float.

Sign of the Crown and the Forge on the right [English Heritage]

17

The MP who went on the tramp

SOME PEOPLE SEEM to live life at ninety miles an hour, as if they know they won't make old bones. Frank Gray of Shipton-on-Cherwell was one of these, helpfully waking weekend guests at his home at Shipton Manor by firing off his gun at 6am, devoting a wing of the house to tramps, standing for election, starting a riot in Oxford, opening a zoo, and driving across Africa—all in just fifty-four years.

A trained solicitor, Gray achieved local celebrity in 1913–14 when he and his friend, motor manufacturer William Morris, campaigned to bring motor buses to Oxford, where the council preferred to stick to

Shipton Manor, Shipton-on-Cherwell

Daimler motorbuses in Cowley Road

trams. At a meeting called to rouse public opinion, Gray made a speech of such incendiary fervour that riots ensued, a tram was overturned and attempts were made to set fire to it. Gray and Morris then went to the Daimler factory and persuaded the company to let them have a couple of buses destined for Salford in Lancashire, the registration "SAL" being replaced with "OX".

Gray's friendships with a chimney sweep, a bookmaker, and other dubious local characters demonstrated his open-minded nature. During the First World War, Gray was exempt from conscription as he was working for the Inland Revenue. But in February 1917 he chose to enlist, recording in his diary: "Tomorrow I go as a conscript to the Army that may be taken to be my position. I go, at all events today anxious to do exactly as the lowest does. I believe I shall find this hard from two standpoints: first I shall be faced with continual temptation to accept something better than others; secondly, my life has had few physical hardship to encounter. On the other hand I have one great help of which

I cannot be deprived, and which outweighs all my disadvantages, that is, that I am by deliberate choice the worst lot which is being forced upon others."

After training, he joined the Oxfordshire and Buckinghamshire Light Infantry and went overseas. Shortly after arriving in France he was posted to Eighth Battalion, the Royal Berkshire Regiment and posted to Number 6 Platoon, B Company. His recollections provide a characteristic insight into the platoon; the captain "had more the appearance of an unsuccessful poet than an officer of the British Army... but his merits, if few, were great". The sergeant was "quite a youth, but one of the smartest little men [Gray] met.'" One of his dearest friends, a clay-digger, was "by his own confession... a keen and successful poacher, with a dash of apple and other petty stealing".

Gray fought in the Third Battle of Ypres, otherwise known as Passchendaele. He was offered a commission and transfer to Transport Command in England, but he refused; he wished to finish the war as he began it, as "Private Gray".

Gray was in the line south of St Quentin on 21 March 1918 when the German Spring Offensive opened. At around 4.30am his battalion was subjected to a heavy bombardment prior to the attack. Gray recalled: "It came and overwhelmed me in an unpausing, irresistible and endless wave of sound. It was caused by the firing of the guns and the bursting of shells and bombs, but in this infernal tornado no discharging gun, no bursting shell or bomb made its individual voice heard above the universal clamour."

Surviving the attack, he was granted leave to England and on his return was appointed to become a clerk in the Intelligence Department of Third Corps Headquarters. Of the role he wrote: "I had expected that this department would provide excitement in war in a much greater degree than it actually did. But, on the other hand, I acquired a knowledge of the general running of an army and of military matters as a

whole beyond my expec-
tations." He remained in
this post until the end of
the war.

His father Sir Walter
Gray had for many years
led the Conservatives on
Oxford County Coun-
cil, but Frank's wartime
experiences made him
an enemy of class privi-
lege. In the general election of 1918 he ran as
the Liberal candidate for
Watford, but he was defeated. In 1920 he was selected as the Liberal
candidate for Oxford City, a seat held by the Conservatives since 1885.
Proving to be a popular figure, he won the seat with a majority of almost
four thousand.

Frank Gray was a smallish man who typically wore a black tie and
black coat with checked trousers and a grey Homburg hat. A colourful
and restless personality, he enlivened one quiet evening by racing a guest
to London, ramming the other man's car when he looked like losing;
then in August 1923, he courted publicity by challenging a fellow MP
to a walking race from Banbury to Oxford in full infantry kit.

He defended his seat in 1923, was re-elected with a reduced majority of 2,693, and rewarded with an appointment as a junior Whip in
the Liberal party. However, he was found to have exceeded his reported
election expenses, and a petition was filed against him in February 1924
for corruption. His young and inexperienced agent, Captain J C John-
stone, was found guilty of corrupt practices. Although Gray's election

was declared void, it was remarked that "his honour remained untarnished". He contested the Portsmouth Central seat in 1924 but was heavily defeated, thus ending his parliamentary career.

Early in 1923, while Gray was still the local MP, members of the brass band at Bletchington, a village across the fields from Gray's home at the manor at Shipton-on-Cherwell, decided to organise a band contest. In order to attract the best bands, the group felt that something special was needed for a trophy for the open section. So band secretary Fred Foreman and the others from Bletchington walked to Shipton Manor hoping for support for their contest—and perhaps even the offer of a fine trophy. Frank Gray agreed to donate a large challenge shield, but asked also that an association be formed of the bands in the area. As a result, the Oxfordshire and District Brass Band Association came into being in April 1923 with Frank Gray as its vice-president.

Soon after his defeat in Portsmouth, the energetic Gray accomplished a remarkable feat of vintage motoring. In 1926 he declared that

Headington Brass Band at the manor, with Gray sitting right of centre

"there was no British car designed for the tropics". The Jowett Company responded, and offered to refund the price of two cars if he succeeded in crossing Africa with them. He accepted, and two standard seven horsepower Jowetts were supplied by the company and fitted with safari bodies; they were duly sign-written "WAIT" and "SEE". Frank Gray and his companion, Jack Sawyer, set off from Lagos on the west coast on 16 March 1926 and in May they arrived at Massawa on the Red Sea, a total distance of about three thousand eight hundred miles. The journey had taken just sixty days, a real accomplishment at that time. At a luncheon provided by the Dunlop Rubber Company to celebrate the success of the journey, Gray reflected on his having fought four elections and served as junior Whip of the Liberal Party and joked: "If such a man is not qualified to face mosquitoes, jungle and swamps, I ask: who is?"

Following the collapse of his parliamentary career, Gray tried unsuccessfully to find work as a miner in Warwickshire in order to expose working conditions. Undeterred, he made a similar and more successful

Gray disguised as a tramp

Bicester workhouse

attempt to experience the life of a tramp in the late nineteen-twenties. After the repeal of the poor law in 1929, he determined to conduct his research personally, donning a disguise, and adopting a change in voice, posture and gait. Remarkably he was not recognised or challenged at any point by a genuine tramp or workhouse official.

He toured the workhouses and casual wards of Oxfordshire. He contributed articles exposing "the workhouse hell" to newspapers, and later published his experiences in 1931 as *The Tramp: His Meaning and Being*. He established The Frank Gray Home for Boys in the former Bicester workhouse in order to help younger vagrants. He also provided a wing at Shipton Manor for the use of those "on the road" and tried to find useful work for them.

In 1928 he helped to establish the *Oxford Mail*, the city's first evening newspaper, and then threw himself into a scheme to develop a zoo, pleasure garden, and associated housing at Kidlington as a gateway to Oxford. The site had earlier been a farmstead and the farm buildings were converted into dens and cages for the animals. There were also large areas for

grazing. *Mail* readers were asked to subscribe to a fund to purchase an elephant, and Rosie became arguably the most famous animal at Oxford Zoo. Animals were given by the London, Berlin, Bristol and Dublin zoos as well as many individual collectors, although some residents that were expected at the opening did not arrive because of an outbreak of foot-and-mouth disease.

The *Oxford Times* reported: "During the last few days, exhibits have been arriving almost hourly and they have settled down in a way that suggests they

Patient Rosie the elephant gave zoo visitors rides

Hanno the lion

have been lifelong inmates. Yesterday, a camel, lion, jackal and two wolves have been put in their quarters and the lion was at once so at home that he enjoyed a long sleep, from which he refused to be awakened by the incessant tapping of workmen's hammers.

"A family of baboons consists of father, mother and three sturdy youngsters, one of which was gravely grooming his grey-bearded father." There were also monkeys, kangaroos, llamas, bears, rabbits, guinea pigs and many birds and fish.

Just five weeks after workmen had first moved in, the zoo was officially opened in July 1931. On the first Sunday, more than two thousand people flocked to the attraction, which included rides on patient Rosie the elephant. Admission was sixpence for adults and three pence for children. Buses were laid on from Oxford.

The zoo made national headlines when three wolves broke through wire netting and escaped. Two were quickly shot dead, but the third vanished and eluded a large team of keepers, police and members of the public for three days. The poor creature was finally cornered and shot in

Harefield House, Summertown: last hide-out of the escaped wolf from Oxford zoo

the grounds of Harefield House, Summertown, by *Oxford Mail* photographer Johnny Johnson.

The zoo had a short life. By August 1936, the organisers were advertising "your last opportunity" to visit. The next month, the whole collection was moved to Dudley Zoo. (Not quite the whole collection—one gentleman who used to help out as a schoolboy remembers taking a goat home on the bus.) Thames Valley Police headquarters now occupies the site and, in 2018, an elephant sculpture was installed on the roundabout at the southern end of Kidlington to commemorate Rosie and the zoo.

Following a period of ill health, and still as fidgety as ever, Gray travelled to South Africa to recuperate. On the return journey he suffered a stroke and died at sea on 3 March 1935. He was buried in Wolvercote cemetery. His coffin was conveyed from Shipton Manor on a flower-bedecked fire engine. After his death, an appreciation of the life of Frank Gray was published in the *Portsmouth Evening News* by one A W Palmer who concluded: "No honours came his way, he was not the sort to get them, but throughout the length and breadth of England there are many who are happier, and better, because Frank Gray came their way."

18

The Sibford hermit

ON THE RARE OCCASIONS upon which reclusive Theodore Lamb chose to utter a few words, an onlooker might have been somewhat disconcerted by the cultured tones in which this striking figure spoke. With all the appearance of a tramp, Theodore in fact came from a good Sibford farming family.

Tall, broad, and strong, Theodore lived in a shack on Sibford Heath, and plied his trade of clock and watch-mending throughout the local villages. His long, matted hair and beard, and his ragged clothes patched together out of

Theodore Lamb

Pupils at the Quaker school carried out domestic tasks to keep the fees manageable

sacking, belied his respectable background and education. He was even said to have mastered several musical instruments.

Born in February 1881 to grazier Joseph John Lamb and his wife Mary Ann Barnes, Theodore went with his siblings to Sibford School, a fee-paying Quaker establishment based at Walford Manor in Main Street, Sibford Ferris. There was a strong tradition of Non-Conformity in the area; a Quaker congregation was established in the village by 1669, when it met in the home of Sibford clockmaker Thomas Gilkes.

A shattering event during Theodore's childhood might account for his later eccentricity. In the autumn of 1887 when Theodore was six years-old, his father Joseph Lamb clambered up into the horse-chestnut tree at the family home, West Town Cottage, to knock down some conkers for the boy. Joseph lost his footing and crashed to the ground, a fall which caused his instant death before the appalled eyes of his son. No child could escape unscathed from such an experience, but whether or not this led to Theodore's reclusive lifestyle cannot be known for certain.

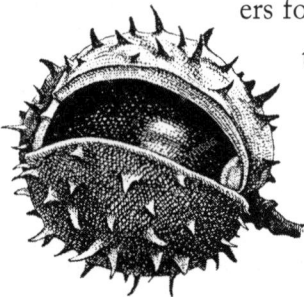

Following Joseph's death, Theodore's mother Mary Ann moved the household to Sibford Gower, a hamlet thick with members of her own Barnes family. Eventually, her brother, widowed chimney sweep Mark Barnes, moved in too.

The next official record we have of Theodore, the 1901 census, reveals his occupation at twenty years old as an "ordinary farm labourer", still living at home with his mother in Sibford Gower. It would be unsurprising if such an intelligent and educated young man found simple farm work unrewarding. At some point, Theodore learned to mend watches and clocks.

North Oxfordshire had been associated with clockmaking since the seventeenth century. Non-Conformists like the Quakers were excluded from the universities and by extension from the professions too so, like the Jews, they had to cultivate their own areas of specialisation. There is no known record of where Theodore learned his trade; he claimed only that he had "picked up" the knowledge here and there.

West Town Cottage in Sibford Ferris: scene of a tragedy in the Lamb family

Romantic disappointment is always the default explanation people fix upon when trying to account for an unconventional life. In Theodore's case, the story goes that the parents of a girl whom he was courting in Chipping Norton prevailed upon her to cut herself off from him. This is said to have broken Theodore's heart and propelled him into eccentricity. Indeed there is a record of banns being read in 1904 of a forthcoming union between one Theodore Lamb and Hannah Godson. However, the couple both claim Lillington in Leamington Spa as their home parish, not Chipping Norton or anywhere in the Banbury area. And Theodore himself told the *Westminster Gazette* in 1926 that he "never thought of marrying". So perhaps the banns referred to a different Theodore.

By 1911, he was living alone at 5 Old Grimsbury Road in Banbury, unmarried and working as a self-employed "watch and clockmaker". According to *Sibford Old Scholars Association* magazine (1950), Theodore was skilful at this work, and was often entrusted by the residents of Banbury with their gold watches and valuable clocks.

Old Grimsbury Road in Banbury

In hospital, Theodore would beg the nurses not to cut off his hair

His classic Victorian terraced cottage at number five was a brick-built two-up, two-down villa with the customary bay-window and recessed front door. His neighbours were chiefly widows and old-age pensioners.

Certainly, he had adopted his unusual appearance by the time he appeared in court aged twenty-five in July 1916 for burning his call-up papers. He pleaded a conscientious objection as a Quaker, and the court explained that he could apply to serve with a non-combatant unit. (The Quakers formed the Friends' Ambulance Unit in 1914.) He was taken to Oxford for his medical, where he reportedly refused to speak a word. He was rejected as unfit for service.

During the First World War, life in a town would not have been comfortable for a young, healthy man who refused to serve. Theodore returned to Sibford, but not into the loving arms of his family. An immensely sturdy man, he hauled a henhouse all the way from Willington, over Brailes Hill and on to Sibford Heath, taking several days over the journey. This was where he intended to live, surrounded by junk and the neat rows of his own vegetable patch.

His neighbours here contrasted not only with the elderly widows of

Theodore stands proudly outside his chicken house

Theodore and his famous bicycle

Old Grimsbury Road, but with one another too: at nearby Heath Farm were dairy farmer Walter Tucker and his wife—to whom, presumably, Theodore paid his two shillings a week rent, and at Tantony Croft were the beautiful Welsh film actress Joyce Bland and her husband John K Carruth, a director of Bentley Motors, Scottish Distillers and others.

Thus commenced three decades of travelling and working around the villages and towns of north Oxfordshire. He used to ride into Banbury on a bicycle devoid of rubber tyres and pulling a crudely-made wooden trolley, filled with pots and lumber. In the town he would buy and sell a few items. In the winter he also carried his fire bucket with him.

He was always totally honest and completely harmless despite his disconcerting appearance. If he called at a house for a glass of water on his wanderings he insisted on paying a penny for it. His clothes were a quaint, homemade garb of sackcloth, although in 1928, when they became rather too quaint, he was fined for inadvertently exposing himself to some startled Banbury ladies. He was banned from the town.

In the same year, he was arrested for begging, and he claimed that he

Theodore was happy to show off to tourists for a few coins

Vine Cottage: home of Theodore's sisters

had not received what was due to him—presumably meaning an inheritance. However, as a younger son of a younger son, it seems unlikely there was much to inherit; Theodore's father Joseph left a personal estate valued at £145 12s 11d, and his brothers all went into trade, not farming.

Theodore was not averse to visitors—indeed coach parties used to include a sight of him on their route—but he had little to say until they dropped a half-crown into his empty tobacco tin. Rationing of some items continued until 1954 in Britain, so the vicar of Sibford Reverend Grogan and his wife would collect Theodore's rations from Banbury every Thursday, and Theodore would pick them up the next day. During bad winter months, he would write messages in the snow if he wanted something, and the villagers would get it for him.

He certainly appears in photographs to be well nourished, and of course three of his sisters still lived nearby to keep an eye on him. Though some Lamb relatives were probably embarrassed by him, suggestions that Theodore was disowned by his entire family seem wide of the mark.

The horse-chestnut tree by the pond at Sibford Gower in 1916

Between the wars his great-nephew Arthur Lamb (1925–1985) used to stay with Theodore's three unmarried sisters Mary, Mildred and Lucretia at Vine Cottage in Bonds End Lane, and Arthur recalled visits to Theodore in his hut during these holidays.

Early in the morning on 21 March 1950, Theodore was found in a distressed condition on the roadside by a bus driver. The previous evening he had set off over the road from his shack to collect water from the spring, but when he tried to climb back up from the gully his legs gave way under him. Forced to spend the night in the open, he contracted pneumonia. He died in Banbury hospital on 23 March 1950 aged sixty-nine, the nurses there respecting his request not to cut off his long hair.

A touching survival from the fateful day of is father Joseph Lamb's death can still be seen. An older cousin, Joshua, was also present and he had the presence of mind to pick up a horse-chestnut from beside Joseph's body. He planted it beside the village pond at Sibford Gower, and the resulting tree flourishes there to this day.

19

The donkey man

"THE DONKEY MAN IS HERE!" For years the excited cry would ring out from children along the route between Banbury and Southam announcing the arrival of Fred Abel's One Man Circus. Travelling entertainer Fred touched the hearts of many when he toured the area in the 1950s, sixties and seventies. Slight, bearded Fred was a familiar sight in his ringmaster's top-hat as he sat outside his caravan surrounded by his beloved dogs, rats, donkeys, and (perhaps inevitably) fleas.

Fred Abel and his colleagues set up camp by the road

With his hoop-topped tent on wheels pulled by two white donkeys, Benjy and Bill, Fred walked along the Oxford-to-Banbury road setting up camp every three or four miles, sometimes just north of Deddington, at other times near the Hopcroft Holt Hotel, Steeple Aston, or near the Shipton-on-Cherwell turn. Inside the mysterious tent, always a source of fascination for children, Fred's possessions consisted simply of a pile of coats to sleep on and a selection of pots and pans. Attractions offered by the circus included donkey rides and a flea circus—in a glass-lidded box in which one particularly talented flea apparently rode a tiny chariot. A stage-struck Jack Russell might easily be persuaded to dance

The performing rats: "Don't force me" could have been Fred's motto too

Towser demonstrates his big finish for ITV

on his back legs, and mice would perform manoeuvres on miniature circus equipment to the tune of *There'll Always Be an England*, scratched out from a wind-up gramophone.

The big finish would be provided by Towser, a giant but docile black Newfoundland dog with a remarkable tolerance for balancing things on his head. Vintage film clips show Towser sitting patiently with a jug on his head, and then parading slowly past his audience while Fred plops one rat after another on to his head and along his back.

Fred was always very polite himself and ticked off children who used bad language. One village lad felt sure that Fred's dusty donkeys must have fleas. When the boy made this accusation to his face, Fred was most offended and went to see the boy's parents who promised to take their rude son to task.

A small, slim-built man who spoke with a pronounced stutter, Fred always looked scruffy. He was friendly and happy to chat, but he would clam up when asked about his background and why he had chosen a life on the road. Apart from his origins in Norfolk, he would give nothing

Far left: 27 Becclesgate in Dereham, Norfolk, where Fred grew up

away, and the usual tale grew up that he must have taken to the travelling life because he had been thwarted in love. This may be partly true.

In fact, Fred was born in 1909 in Dereham in the Brecklands of Norfolk where his father John was a furnace-man in an iron foundry. Fred's mother Rose died when he was twelve, his father when he was seventeen, so thereafter Fred was on his own. By 1939 he was lodging with a couple in Ipswich and working as a labourer in a heavy engineering works. At the age of thirty-two in 1941, Fred married Ivy Green, twenty-five, a local girl who worked in a ladies' silk-underwear factory. In the following year the couple had a daughter.

When war broke out, claimed the *Oxford Times* in 1982, Fred joined the Royal Artillery. Towards the end of the war his gun-site was, it is said, hit by a bomb, burying Fred under heaps of rubble. His jaw was smashed, rendering speech difficult. The *Birmingham Daily Post* reported in 1961 that he had been invalided out of the army. Whatever the accuracy of these reports, Fred himself admitted to the same newspaper in 1966: "I was bombed, I was. I don't talk about it.

"My speech holds me up sometimes and my nerves have gone. And

Fred and his donkeys engage in a discussion about which route to take

I can't hold a razor. I didn't really want a beard you know. But I have it trimmed sometimes, and we get on very well."

In the years after Fred came home, his marriage to Ivy collapsed, leaving him homeless. With his parents both long dead, plus his own inability to stick to the regular employment that would enable him to pay rent on a home, Fred had little choice but to opt for a life on the road with his animal friends. It is not unknown for those who are disillusioned by the faithlessness of humans to find the loyalty and friendship of animals more reliable.

As it turned out, Fred became a much-loved figure in the area, with people keen to help him wherever he went. He was a welcome visitor at Oathill Farm in Cropredy where he would stay at the bottom of the drive and come up to the house to perform for the Cullimore children. Every day he would enjoy tea, sandwiches and cake, and indulge in a good natter with Norfolk-born Mrs Cullimore as they reminisced about places they both knew.

Mary Churchill in Cosy Lane in Deddington, where Fred often parked up, would fill his water cans and give him a cooked meal, even sometimes a Sunday roast. Always dignified in his gratitude, he would invariably say: "Thank you ma'am, ta." When Fred set up camp in Clifton, Gerald French would give him a free hair-cut, and Gerald's wife Violet would provide him with hot meals. He had simple tastes though, and was just as happy with bread and cheese.

In 1965, a hit-and-run motorist demolished Fred's "wheely tent" leaving him and his circus of animals homeless. His friends quickly collected enough money to buy him a brand new three-wheeled cart on which was painted in brave white letters: "FRED ABEL'S CIRCUS", and underneath in smaller capitals, "AS SEEN ON TV". The outside of this mobile tent also announced: "NO TV, NO TAX", indicating to those with thieving tendencies that he carried no valuables.

However, because of his eccentricity, his raggedy appearance and his general defencelessness, he attracted the attention of trouble-makers who became convinced that he must be a rich old fool who just might have a lot of money hidden in his cart. In 1975 the *Coventry Evening Telegraph* reported that Fred's caravan had been raided by thieves who had stolen what savings he had scraped together over the years to buy himself a proper caravan.

Deddington in the sixties

Tadmarton House: Fred spent his final years in an outbuilding here

The story so touched the hearts of the people who knew Fred that an appeal launched by Sir George Beaumont of Deddington soon raised more than the reported two hundred pounds that had been stolen. A year later friends from Tadmarton House Farm and Deddington Mill helped him buy a comfortable caravan complete with bunk bed, curtains and even a fitted carpet.

As he grew older he no longer moved very far from Deddington where he maintained his old trusted friendships with the families who had always welcomed him, given him the odd meal, and even coaxed him into having a bath. Fred was persuaded to give up the travelling life and Colonel Lewis from Tadmarton renovated a large chicken house on his farm in which Fred lived happily until 1979. Passers-by dropped off clothes and food or left them for him at the police house.

Fred never threw anything away and the inside of his caravan grew less and less sweet smelling. For Fred, with his health broken and his roving spirit denied, old age spelt trouble. The local bobby, PC Rampley, regularly stopped by on his beat to keep an eye on Fred—at least, as often as Fred's protective dogs would allow him near.

One day PC Rampley felt sure that Fred was inside his caravan, but he couldn't see him. Once the RSPCA inspector had managed to remove Fred's dogs, the ambulance crew standing by were able to examine him. Fred had suffered a major stroke which left him unable to move or speak. He was taken to the Horton Hospital, where doctors soon realised that he would need to live out his life in the care of kind medical staff.

Fred never fully recovered. The RSPCA took charge of his dogs and Sir George gave Benjy and Bill a home at his wife's donkey stud. At the hospital, because he had been outdoors all his life Fred was given a bit of privacy, with a corner of the ward to himself. His friends from Deddington Mill, who had taken charge of his donkeys, brought them to the ward window where Fred could greet them from his wheelchair. He died in February 1982 at the age of seventy-two.

This modest, kind man who used to bring so much joy to the area's children on his travels would surely be most gratified that those same children, now well into middle age, still remember the name of his dog and treasure every faded photograph of him they possess.

He has become the symbol of a simpler age when mothers happily gave their children tuppence to scramble off unaccompanied to enjoy the flea circus, in spite of the chance that the odd performer might hitch a ride home. Boys and girls would beg indulgent mothers for sausages to share a fry-up with Fred, no matter how unhygienic his cooking utensils, and a ride on one of his donkeys was a pleasure never to be forgotten.

One wonders what modern society would make of Fred Abel doing his own thing in twenty-first-century Oxfordshire. His stubborn independence against all odds is a precious memory.

Fred, the donkey man with the roving spirit, was cremated at Oxford Crematorium and his ashes were borne by the winds into the country-side he loved.

20
The worker-priest

WHEN THE LORD MAYOR of Oxford toured the Thames Water treatment works at Swinford in the early 1980s, nervous bosses ordered employees to stand well back and keep quiet. Apprentice Tim Siret did as he was told. But the mayor, glancing across and catching Tim's eye, strode over and boomed cheerfully: "Aren't you Charlie Siret's lad?"

"You could have cut the atmosphere with a knife," recalls Tim, son of notorious Communist trouble-maker Charlie Siret. "We'd met at a demo somewhere. I'll never forget the bosses' faces—pure horror!" But

they needn't have worried because this mayor was a bit different. He was Tony Williamson, fork-lift truck driver, workers' champion, anti-racism campaigner, and clergyman.

Tony was born in Fenny Drayton, Leicestershire, in 1933. He was the youngest of three children of Anglican minister Joe Williamson

Tony Williamson

Oxford University in the fifties

("Father Joe") and Audrey. Joe, who was brought up in poverty in London's East End, was well known in the 1950s as a campaigner for slum clearance, for opening refuges for prostitutes, and for merrily antagonising the church hierarchy into the bargain. If all this brings to mind a certain character in the television drama *Call the Midwife*, it is hardly surprising because "Tom Hereward", reverend of Poplar, was indeed based on Father Joe. Tony inherited Joe's determination to fight injustice.

During Britain's post-war boom, Tony felt that the church was ignoring the alienation of ordinary workers. In 1958, as an idealistic graduate of Trinity College, Oxford, he clocked on as a fork-lift truck driver at the Pressed Steel car-body factory in Cowley, now the home of the Mini. His first year was spent unloading press-shop panels, and then he spent a year driving a press-shop tractor. In June 1960 he was ordained deacon in the Church of England. He was now a worker-priest—the first-ever Anglican priest to be ordained while employed in factory work.

Worker-priests originated in the French Catholic church in the 1940s. Frustrated by the gulf between ordinary people and their tradition-bound church, hundreds of Roman Catholic priests had chosen to work in French factories and to conduct their ministry from there. In the Second World War, dozens of French worker-priests secretly joined compatriots forced to work in German arms factories; some perished in Nazi concentration camps.

Even in peace-time, being a worker-priest meant sharing with ordinary people the experience of having little control over working conditions, experiencing exhaustion from physical labour, and dealing with the shock when your workplace was closed or "restructured", with its attendant unemployment and insecurity.

Soon after entering the factory, Tony became a Transport and General Workers' Union representative on the canteens committee and later he helped senior union colleagues with paperwork and record keeping. Tony acknowledged that his middle-class background meant he lacked an instinctive feel for leading union campaigns, yet his commitment and organisational skills proved assets for local union leaders.

The management at Pressed Steel, on the other hand, felt that, in his newly-dignified position as a clergyman, Tony should now become a white-collar worker. Tony declined, expressing a desire to remain alongside his fellow workers once he was ordained. He explained later: "I felt I should stay on the shop floor as there was a constant feel of nearness to everyday man." With the support of the then-Bishop of Oxford, the Right Reverend Harry Carpenter, and the agreement of Pressed Steel management, he was allowed to do so.

His workmates treated him as a colleague and he saw his worker-priest role as solving practical problems. In a 1961 sermon he said: "Instead of being an individual of the utmost value to God… I am one of twelve thousand [Oxford car factory] employees, each easily replaceable. My clock number is 261092." Tony would continue to drive fork-lift trucks for thirty years, clocking on daily at 7.15am.

As soon as Tony was ordained, the outside world began to take an interest in this unfamiliar combination—a priest working as a fork-lift driver. Press and television coverage followed. Residents in Dodgson Road in Cowley were amused to observe television cameras filming

Tony cycling home from work—over and over again. The camera crew required multiple retakes, and Tony was late home for tea that day.

At the end of 1960, Tony was among fifteen hundred Pressed Steel workers made redundant, so he spent three months

The Williamson family home in Dodgson Road, Cowley

Many Pressed Steel workers could not afford the cars they helped to make

driving a laundry van round the villages of Oxfordshire. He was recalled to the factory in April 1961, and shortly afterwards he stood as a Labour candidate for Oxford City Council, enjoying success at the first attempt.

In 1971 he was elected chairman of the six-thousand-member Pressed Steel 5/60 branch of the Transport and General Workers' Union at a time of industrial conflict and industry decline. Asked how he reconciled the church and socialism, he replied: "I have never seen any demarcation line because they are both concerned with people's well-being."

Bad politics, he explained, is promising things that cannot be delivered. He believed that local councils were very important, so Christians should be in the thick of it and try to work out the best possible solutions. Tony saw himself always as a representative of people, whichever role he was in at the time.

At the height of a labour dispute in 1971, the *Sun* newspaper described him as "one of the toughest and most remarkable trade union leaders in Britain". The paper quoted one of the factory bosses as saying,

"He's always very polite but completely dedicated to his men. It takes a box of gelignite to move him an inch."

By the 1960s, tens of thousands of people from the Commonwealth had settled in Oxford, filling labour shortages in industry and the public sector, giving the city a multicultural identity rather earlier than elsewhere. In early 1962, the government tabled the Commonwealth Immigration Bill, designed heavily to limit immigration from the former colonies of the Commonwealth. People from many walks of life in Oxford opposed the Bill.

Various pressure groups emerged to promote racial integration and anti-racism, and on Sunday 4 February 1962 those opposing the Bill marched through the city centre under the banner of the Movement for Colonial Freedom, rallying outside St John's College in St Giles.

Canon Tony Williamson was a freshly-elected member of Oxford City Council at the time, and he used this platform to speak out. The *Oxford Mail* reported: "Mr Williamson, waving a copy of the Bill, told an audience of about two hundred people: 'We have got to see that we get over this problem without making coloured people scapegoats. We cannot build our council houses in Oxford because we have not got enough labour. We have three thousand jobs waiting and yet we say, 'No, you cannot come in.'"

Despite this protest and others across the country, this particular battle was lost; the Bill became law in July that year and conflicts over race and racism continued. In one case an Indian man, Hans Raj Gupta, was the victim of a racist attack outside his home only months after he had been recognised as the first Indian to reach the rank of bus inspector in Oxford.

Elsewhere, dozens of protesters were arrested for occupying Annette's hair salon in Cowley Road after staff refused to cut the hair of black and Asian customers. And dozens more were detained when Enoch Powell, the far-right politician, came to speak at Oxford Town Hall.

Annette's hairdressing salon: employees refused to cut the hair of black clients

This was the period during which Tony Williamson's focus centred most on anti-racism work. He chaired the Oxford Committee for Racial Integration (OCRI), a pioneering anti-racist community organisation set up in 1965. OCRI warned of the rise of the extreme right, and their Cowley Road offices were vandalised.

In 1965 a decision by Oxford police stirred such a controversy that it reached the Home Office and the House of Commons. Immigration officers blocked Ghulam Shabir, a fifteen-year-old Pakistani boy, from entering

OCRI HQ in Cowley Road, Oxford

the UK to join family members in Oxford because local police pronounced that the family was living in overcrowded conditions.

Shocked by this, Williamson researched the facts of the case for himself and found that the claim was quite untrue. He presented his findings to Oxford police and council officials, and his efforts contributed to an abrupt police climb-down, and an admission that the original report was inaccurate. In full retreat, the Home Office allowed young Ghulam to re-apply for an entry permit to the UK.

Tony took a year's paid leave to be Lord Mayor of Oxford in 1982-83, and this was when the encounter with Charlie Siret's son at the Swinford waterworks occurred. After 1983 his County Council responsibilities meant spending less time in the factory. But he continued with his fork-lift driving, as well as working in the stores and even sticking masking tape on Rover-800 bumpers.

Since 1958 Tony had continued to celebrate services at St Luke's Church in Cowley every Wednesday morning at 6.30am and often on Sunday, and took services and preached at other times and places

As mayor of Oxford, Tony attended the annual Port Meadow inspection

Blackbird Leys was built to house the car workers Tony knew so well

as required. He also took on the duties of clerk to the Blackbird Leys neighbourhood council. As if this weren't enough, he conducted baptisms, weddings and funerals for those who had no tie with any particular church, and became the first chair of BBC Radio Oxford from 1970 to 1974. Hardly surprisingly, in view of that little lot, in 1977 he was appointed OBE. After leaving Pressed Steel in 1987, Tony's major role was education spokesman for the Labour group on the County Council.

Eventually, he served as an innovative director of education for the Diocese of Oxford, in charge of a team supporting two hundred and seventy church schools in Berkshire, Buckinghamshire and Oxfordshire. He introduced the first Service Level Agreement with schools, then known as the Zebedee Scheme. Now almost three hundred schools subscribe to the diocese's SLA which allows the diocese to provide them with high levels of support across all areas of school life.

"He was imaginative in changing things and getting things done," says Gordon Joyner, deputy director of education, who was appointed by Tony in 1993. "He just had enormous amounts of integrity. I always

In later years, Tony revisits the former TGWU HQ in Cowley Road

remember he said if you go into a situation or school and something has gone wrong, say you have made a mistake, hold your hands up and move forward. It disarms the situation."

After leaving Pressed Steel, Tony settled with his wife Barbara in Watlington. Even as he battled cancer in his final years, he threw himself in to organising a million things as well as continuing to lead worship. He joked that the only thing missing from his busy schedule was his departure date. In fact he died in 2019, having been made an honorary alderman, Oxford County Council's highest honour, two years before his death.

Sources

Chapter 1: The reluctant rector
steepleastonarchive.org.uk
Anthony Wood, *Athenae Oxonienses*, volume 3, p 794
Richard Duckworth, *Tintinnalogia—or the Art of Ringing, &c*, Fabian Stedman (1668)
"Duckworth, Richard (bap. 1631?, d. 1706), writer on campanology", by James
    McMullen Rigg, *Dictionary of National Biography, 1885-1900*, volume 16
theclergydatabase.org.uk

Chapter 2: The Woodstock pirate
"Uncovered: the man behind Coleridge's Ancient Mariner", Vanessa Thorp,
    Guardian, 31 Jan 2010,
England & Wales, Prerogative Court of Canterbury Wills, 1384-1858, Simonis
    Hatley, PROB II/530
George Shelvocke, *A Voyage Round the World by Way of the Great South Sea (1726)*,
    pp 72–73
Robert Fowke, *The Real Ancient Mariner*, (Travelbrief, 2010)

Chapter 3: The fortunate cooper
Jackson's Oxford Journal, 25 Sept 1819
England & Wales, Prerogative Court of Canterbury Wills, 1384-1858, John Allder,
    PROBII/1066
A True Copy of the Poll Book Oxford (1768)
" John Alder, the lucky cooper", *www.abingdon.gov.uk*
"Abingdon Racecourse", *www.greyhoundderby.com*

Chapter 4: The mock candidate
Jackson's Oxford Journal, 18 March 1820; 11 June 1831
Oxford University, City, and County Herald, 29 May 1841
Banbury Guardian, 5 June 1841, 26 December 1889
Oxford University, City, and County Herald, 12 June 1841
Keith Chandler, "A Very Celebrated Banbury Character: reconstructing working class
    biography—the case of William 'Old Mettle' Castle", *Cake & Cockhorse* (Banbury
    Historical Society), volume 15, number 1, Autumn/Winter 2000
Michael Heaney, "With Scarfes and Garters as You Please: an exploratory Essay in
    the Economics of the Morris", *Folk Music Journal*, volume 6, number 4 (1993),
    pp 491-505
Sarah Beesley, *My life*, (printed for private circulation, 1892)

Christiana S Cheney (ed), George Herbert, *Shoemaker's Window: Recollections of a Midland Town before the Railway Age*, (Blackwell, 1949)

P Reynold (ed), *Banbury Gaol Records* (Banbury Historical Society, 1987)

Chapter 5: The hungry palaeontologist

"Buckland, William (1784–1856), geologist and dean of Westminster", Neville Haile, *Oxford Dictionary of National Biography*

"Learning more: William Buckland", *www.oum.ox.ac.uk*

Walter Bruno Gratzer, *Eurekas and Euphorias: The Oxford Book of Scientific Anecdotes*, OUP, 2002

Report and Transactions: The Devonshire Association for the Advancement of Science, Literature and Art (1933) p 409

Gordon, Elizabeth Oke, *The life and correspondence of William Buckland, DD, FRS*, pp 267–268 (J Murray, 1894)

Chapter 6: The Banbury pedestrian

Oxford University and City Herald, 10 February 1816; 16 April 1816

Oxford Chronicle, 24 Dec 1859

"The Plush Industry in Shutford", Vera Hodgkins, *Cake and Cockhorse* (Banbury Historical Society), volume 6, number 3, Autumn 1975

"Banbury's Poor in 1850", Barrie S Trinder, *Cake and Cockhorse* (Banbury Historical Society), volume 3, number 6, Winter 1966

"A Hook Norton Family: the Calcotts", Sue Coltman, *Cake and Cockhorse* (Banbury Historical Society), volume 96, number 1, Autumn 1982

"Banbury Charities", C Crouch, *Cake and Cockhorse* (Banbury Historical Society), volume 11, number 1, Autumn 1988

"Banbury's Village: What Remains of Neithrop ", Steve Kilsby, *Cake and Cockhorse* (Banbury Historical Society), volume 20, number 6, Summer 2017

Chapter 7: The body-snatcher of Bodicote

Jackson's Oxford Journal, 22 October 1831; 7 Jan 1832

A W Pain, "Banbury Gaol Records 1829–1838", *Cake and Cockhorse* (Banbury Historical Society), volume 2, number 11, January 1965

"The Bodicote Bodysnatchers", *Cake and Cockhorse* (Banbury Historical Society), volume 3, number 7, Spring 1967

Chapter 8: The gypsy who built a house

Jackson's Oxford Journal, 18 November 1826; 7 May 1836

"Sineta Lambourne and Sineta Smith", E O Winstedt, *Journal of the Gypsy Lore Society*, series 3 volume 23-24 1944/1945

"A Manuscript History of Summertown," H Minn, *Oxoniensa*, volume 11–12, p 152 (1946)

"Early Modern Oxford", *A History of the County of Oxford: Volume 4, the City of Oxford,* ed. Alan Crossley and C R Elrington (eds) (London, 1979), pp. 74-180

George Smith, *Gipsy Life: being an Account of our Gipsies and their Children with Suggestions for their Improvement* (Haughton & Co, 1880)

Joanne Major, Sarah Murden, *A Right Royal Scandal: Two Marriages That Changed History,* (Pen & Sword, 2026)

England & Wales, Prerogative Court of Canterbury Wills, 1384-1858, John Lambourn, PROBII/1942

Chapter 9: The transported convict

Jackson's Oxford Journal, 29 October 1818

Berkshire Chronicle, 1 March 1828

oldbaileyonline.org

freesettlerorfelon.com

convictrecords.com.au

australianroyalty.net.au

Chapter 10: The real mad hatter

Jackson's Oxford Journal, 21 May 1864; 24 September 1887

"Oxford History: Mayors & Lord Mayors: Thomas Randall", *oxfordhistory.org.uk*

"Thomas Randall and Grandpont House", Mark Davies, *southoxfordhistory.org.uk*

England & Wales, National Probate Calendar (Index of Wills and Administrations), 1858-1995, Thomas Randall

Chapter 11: The ghost of Church Hanborough

Jackson's Oxford Journal, 31 Aug 1844; 4 Nov 1848; 24 Apr 1852; 12 May 1855; 30 May 1857; 6 Jun 1857; 20 Feb 1864

Eastwood, David. "Communities, Protest and Police in Early Nineteenth-Century Oxfordshire: The Enclosure of Otmoor Reconsidered", *The Agricultural History Review,* vol 44, number 1, 1996, pp 35–46

Chapter 12: The duelling vicar

Melbourne Argus, 18 May 1847

Jackson's Oxford Journal, 15 Apr 1887

The Australasian, 16 March 1940

"Fire! The Duel at Cape Schanck", Peter McCullough, *Peninsula Essence,* August 2017, pp 66– 72

"The Early History of the Mornington Peninsula", Hunter Rogers, *Mornington*

Leader, 1960

Jeremy Hales and Marion le Cheminant, *The Letters of Henry Howard Meyrick: May 1840– November 1841 and January 1845–April 1847,* (JJB Publishing, 1997)

Frederick James Meyrick, *Life in the Bush 1840–1847: A memoir of Henry Howard Meyrick,* (T Nelson and Sons, 1939)

Paul de Serville, *Port Phillip Gentlemen and good society in Melbourne before the gold rushes* (Oxford University Press, 1980)

"Edward Barker, John Barker, Redmond Barry, Peter Snodgrass", *Australian Dictionary of Biography*

Chapter 13: The good soldier

Jackson's Oxford Journal, 31 July 1875; 6 Dec 1876; 30 Dec 1876; 25 Oct 1879; 10 May 1884; 30 Aug 1884; 14 Mar 1885; 1 Jan 1887; 23 Apr 1887; 17 Sept 1887; 7 Jul 1888; 1 Sept 1888; 21 Jun 1890

Police Gazette, 14 Mar 1890

British Army Service Records WO97/1463/032

Chapter 14: The Bampton inventor

Graham Newman, *Mr Onesiphorus Oliver Collett and the 'Bampton Voiturette',* (issuu. com, 10 May 2020)

"Clanfield Colletts", *clanfield.yolasite.com*

Chapter 15: The Attagirl

"Obituary of Freydis Sharland (190–2014)", *bensingtonhistory.org*

"Ordinary People, Extraordinary Lives", *Candia* online magazine

"First Officer Freydis Sharland: Veteran of wartime Air Transport Auxiliary who braved hazardous conditions to deliver Spitfires", Anne Keleny, *Independent,* 24 July 2014

"Unsung' angel who flew fighter planes for the RAF dies aged 103", Harry Howard, *Daily Mail,* 26 August 2022

"Freydis Sharland, née Leaf, ATA pilot", *war-experience.org*

Chapter 16: The wartime decoy

"The Night that the Germans bombed Upton", Mike Brown, 9 March 2011, *uptonvillage.co.uk*

Neil R Storey, *Norfolk in the second world war* (Halsgrove, 2010)

Chapter 17: The MP who went on the tramp

The Times, 4 March 1935

Western Gazette, 21 February 1930

Charles Fenby, *The other Oxford: the life and times of Frank Gray and his father* (Lund Humphries, 1970)

Chapter 18: The Sibford hermit
Banbury Advertiser, 26 June 1913
Banbury Guardian, 8 July 1916; 20 July 1916; 30 Aug 1928; 23 Mar 1950;
23 Mar 1950; 30 Mar 1950
Birmingham Daily Gazette, 24 Mar 1950
Northampton Mercury, 28 April 1939
Warwick and Warwickshire Advertiser, 30 April 1948
Westminster Gazette, 14 October 1926
Sibford Old Scholars Association magazine, 1950
"Theodore Lamb (1880–1950)", *thesibfords.uk*

Chapter 19: The donkey man
Birmingham Daily Post, 21 February 1961; 6 October 1966
Coventry Evening Telegraph, 7 April 1975
Oxford Times, 5 February 1982
Banbury Guardian, 8 Aug 2002
"Fred Abel (the Donkey Man)", Rob Forsyth, 25 March 2016, *deddingtonhistory.uk*
"Fred Abel—one of life's characters", *southamheritage.org*

Chapter 20: The worker-priest
Information provided to the author by the Siret family
Oxford Mail, 1 April 2021
"The Rev Tony Williamson obituary", Hugh Williamson, *Guardian,* 28 Feb 2019
"Tony Williamson, ex-Lord Mayor of Oxford", James Roberts, *Oxford Mail,*
21 February 2019
"Tony Williamson: life of a trade unionist", Hugh Williamson, 1 July 1 2019,
hughwilliamson.org

Also by Julie Ann Godson

THE WATER GYPSY
How a Thames fishergirl became a viscountess
AT DUSK on a snowy evening in 1766 a tired young couple made out the welcoming lights burning in the windows of creaky old Shellingford Manor in the Vale of the White Horse, the house that was to be their home. He was Viscount Ashbrook, she was Betty Ridge, daughter of a humble Thames fisherman. Earlier that day they had been married in a little village church, and now Betty—a real-life Cinderella—was embarking on a new life in the alien world of the aristocracy.

SCANDAL IN HIGH SOCIETY OXFORDSHIRE
Twenty tales of toffs in trouble
SECRET LOVE AFFAIRS, murder, poisoning and extortion—this book tells twenty tales of Oxfordshire toffs in trouble, from Tudor times up to the modern age. Few will fail to be impressed by the sheer variety of ways in which the upper classes of the county contrived over the centuries to behave disgracefully.

OUR BOYS 1914–1918
Who were the fallen of one Oxfordshire valley?
FROM THE WORKHOUSE boy who became an early submariner to the officer who proved to be not quite such a gentleman after all, forty-eight men from the Lower Windrush Valley in Oxfordshire are listed on the First World War memorials there. This book attempts to provide a glimpse of them in the villages, farms, and lanes where they lived and worked—with their families, plying a trade, or labouring in the fields.

ON THIS DAY IN OXFORDSHIRE
PICK ANY DAY of the year, and something interesting will have happened somewhere in Oxfordshire. The county has experienced its share of events of national importance: rioting, civil war, archaeological finds and life-changing inventions. At the same time, ordinary people have struggled through their own dramas, sometimes with only alcohol to soothe their fears. This book offers a daily snapshot of their lives from the seventh century through to modern times.

1066: OXFORDSHIRE & THE NORMAN CONQUEST
Why it all started and finished in our county
IT WAS AN EVENT which changed the country forever. And from the birth of a prince to the formal surrender after the Battle of Hastings, Oxfordshire frequently provided the background for the board-room take-over which was the Norman Conquest of England.

Available on Amazon • www.julieanngodson.com

Printed in Great Britain
by Amazon

17253968R00119